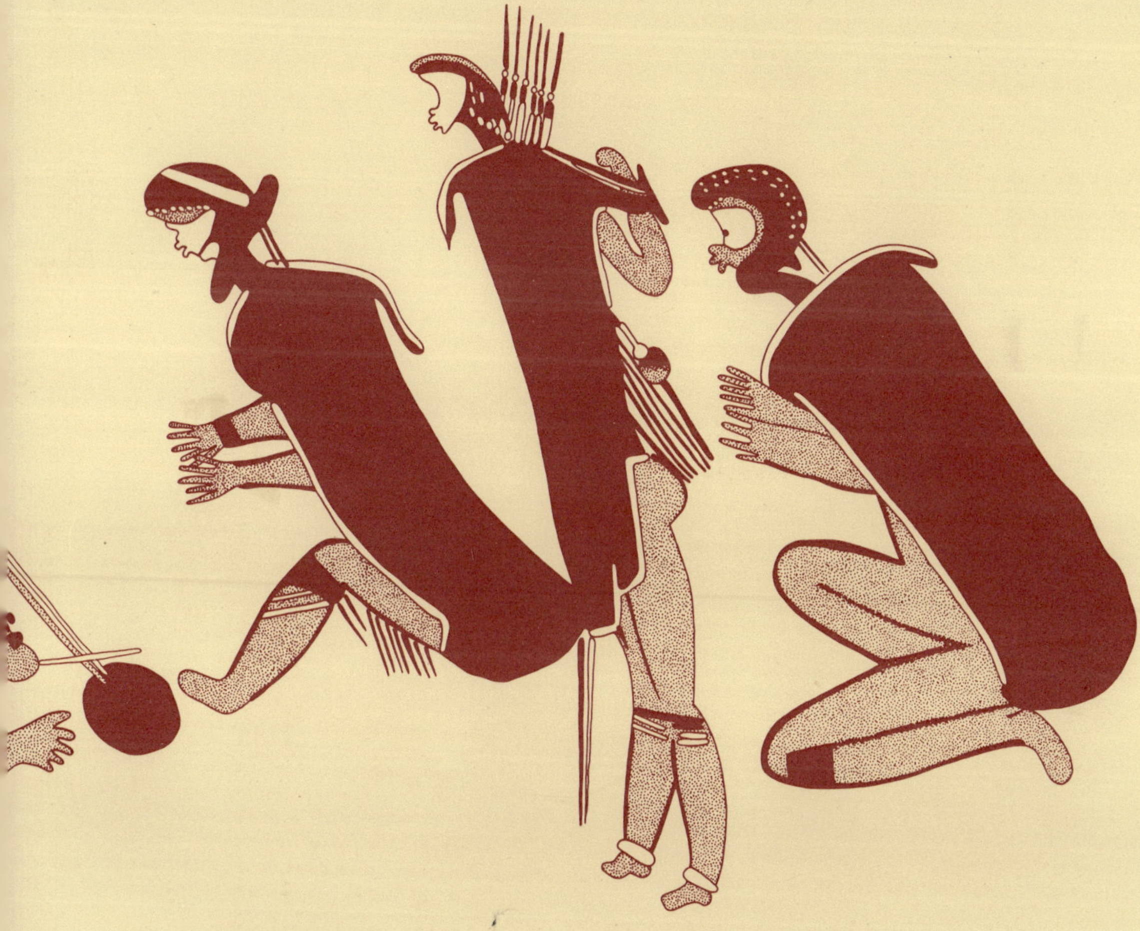

IMAGES OF POWER

IMAGES OF POWER

UNDERSTANDING BUSHMAN ROCK ART
David Lewis-Williams · Thomas Dowson

SOUTHERN
BOOK PUBLISHERS

Copyright © 1989 by J.D. Lewis-Williams and T.A. Dowson

All rights reserved. No part of this publication may be reproduced or transmitted in any form or by any means without prior written permission from the publisher

ISBN 1 86812 196 8

First edition, first impression 1989

Published by
Southern Book Publishers (Pty) Ltd
P.O. Box 548, Bergvlei 2012
Johannesburg

Jacket design by Michael Barnett

Layout by Designaline

Set in 11 on 13 pt Hanover
by Unifoto, Cape Town

Black/white and two colour sections printed on
115 gsm Dukuza matt
Full colour section printed on 115 gsm Dukuza gloss

Printed and bound by
National Book Printers, Cape

ACKNOWLEDGEMENTS

In writing this book, we have become indebted to a great many people. Over the years, farmers in different parts of southern Africa have given up their time to take us to sites and have given us permission to camp on their property. We have withheld their names and the names of their farms to protect the sites on their land from vandalism, but our debt to them is enormous. We are as greatly indebted to the Natal Parks Board and its officers responsible for the Drakensberg reserves. The Natal Parks Board and other parks boards have done much to protect rock art sites. We thank students and past members of the Rock Art Research Unit, especially Paul den Hoed, who assisted greatly with fieldwork. Dr Lorna Marshall kindly allowed us to use two of her photographs. Dr A.S.C. Hooper, the Librarian, Jagger Library, University of Cape Town, permitted quotation from the Bleek Collection and, through the good offices of Ms L. Twentyman-Jones and Ms E. Eberhardt, provided photographs of Wilhelm Bleek and a page from one of Lucy Lloyd's notebooks. Mrs W. Job, Department of Geography, University of the Witwatersrand, assisted with the maps. Mrs S.A. Pager generously allowed us to use her late husband's copy of the 'White Lady of the Brandberg'. Dr A.D. Mazel provided 39b. Throughout the preparation of this book, we have benefited from discussions with other members of the Rock Art Research Unit and the Department of Archaeology, University of the Witwatersrand. Professor T.N. Huffman, Dr J. Deacon, Professor P. Bonner, Dr L. Wadley, Mr M. Taylor and Mr B. Michael kindly read and commented on drafts of the manuscript. The Rock Art Research Unit is funded by the Institute for Research Development of the Human Sciences Research Council and the University of the Witwatersrand. The opinions expressed and the conclusions arrived at are the authors' and are not necessarily to be attributed to either institution. Ms M. Ramsay kindly typed the manuscript in its successive versions.

PREFACE

Since the turn of the century a great deal of archaeological attention has focused on Upper Palaeolithic art in such famous French and Spanish caves as Lascaux and Altamira. This art, made between approximately 10 and 35 thousand years ago, is recognised as the oldest depictions made by human beings. Throughout the century since its discovery the world has marvelled at its beauty and debated its meaning. Why did people all those millennia ago walk, climb and crawl for hundreds of kilometres underground to make pictures of bison, horses, reindeer and strange geometric signs? Were these first fully modern human beings performing a religious rite? Were they propitiating the gods of the underworld?

While archaeologists were wrestling with these daunting questions, they tended to overlook another rock art that had in fact been known for as much as a century before the discovery of Upper Palaeolithic art. In the rock shelters and on the open hilltops of southern Africa there are hundreds of thousands of paintings and rock engravings, many of them done in astonishing detail and, apparently, depicting more aspects of daily life than the Upper Palaeolithic art. Yet this art has never engaged the archaeological imagination with the same intensity as Upper Palaeolithic art. Why?

One reason is that the southern African artists were well known: they were the Bushmen, a race despised and considered by many Westerners to be on the lowest rungs of human evolution. How, archaeologists reasoned, could such primitive people produce anything of interest? Surely their art can be no more than naive daubings, perhaps the product of some primeval urge to leave marks on their surroundings. Misgivings such as these did not encourage archaeologists to give serious attention to Bushman rock art.

Then there was a further discouraging factor. Archaeologists saw the French and Spanish art as the handiwork of their own ancient ancestors, Europe's great aesthetic gift to the world. By contrast, southern Africa was a human backwater in which a totally foreign and primitive people led a stultifying life without a future and incapable of civilized development. Nothing of great interest to be had there!

Now, at last, world opinion is changing. Bushman rock art is becoming recognised as one of the great achievements of humankind. It is an art of striking complexity, both intellectual and aesthetic. Not only does it match the more famous Upper Palaeolithic art, but its symbolism and subtlety can readily be discussed alongside any of the great periods of Western art. The work of the Italian Renaissance painters and sculptors, the Flemish masters and the French Impressionists is no more 'advanced' or intricate than Bushman rock art.

This is a bold claim and one that will surprise, even shock, many people, but this book aims to go some way towards justifying it. Twenty years ago rock art researchers were pioneering a new kind of archaeological thinking that is only now being adopted by archaeologists in general: we try to achieve an 'insider's view'. In other words, we try, as best we can, to see the art through Bushman eyes. What did the artists themselves believe about the cavalcade of animals that traverses the rocks of southern Africa? What strange actions, perhaps rituals, are the animated human figures performing? When we adopt this approach, we find that all the 'simplicity' and 'primitiveness' is a mirage. The haze of prejudice lifts, and we see, by means of the art, into the heart of Bushman religious experience. The great theme of Bushman art is the power of animals to sustain and transform human life by affording access to otherwise unattainable spiritual dimensions.

Today research is coming full-circle. Armed with what we know about Bushman religious experience and the ways in which it is emblazoned on the rocks of southern Africa, we are returning to the dark caverns of western Europe. Contrary to the received archaeological wisdom of decades, we are finding that important clues to the great enigmas of Upper Palaeolithic art have been awaiting discovery in an entirely unexpected place: southern Africa. How those clues are unlocking Upper Palaeolithic mysteries previously thought impenetrable is, of course, another story. Here we are concerned with the great efflorescence of Bushman art itself. But we outline our new understanding of this art in the exciting knowledge that it points to the very origin of artistic activity and thence to some of humankind's greatest triumphs. Bushman rock art stands at the centre of research into the origins of religion and aesthetics.

Few, if any, of the understandings this book offers would have been possible without, first, the work of Wilhelm Bleek, Lucy Lloyd and J.M. Orpen in the 1870s and, secondly, the modern researches of anthropologists in the Kalahari Desert. These people not only provided vital insights into Bushman belief and ritual, but also brought the Bushmen themselves and their terrible plight to the attention of the world. The doyen of the twentieth century workers is Dr Lorna Marshall. She, her late husband Laurence, her son John and her daughter Elizabeth first went into the Kalahari in 1950. Combining research with compassion, they have kept up their concern for the Bushmen to this day. At all times Lorna Marshall and many other researchers have generously assisted and encouraged us with our work on Bushman rock art. That is why we dedicate this book to them and to the humanitarian cause they serve so faithfully.

J.D.L-W.
T.A.D.
May 1989

For
Lorna Marshall
and
*all the other workers who have done
so much for the Kalahari Bushmen*

CONTENTS

PART I
The Bushmen and their art   1
Who were the artists?   4
The Bushmen   8
Way of life   11
Bushman religion   13
Distribution of Bushman rock art   13
Technique   18
   Paintings   18
   Engravings   19
   Learning the techniques   20
The age of the art   20
What does the art mean?   23
   Older interpretations   23
   Bushmen beliefs   26
   Recent research   30

PART II
Detailed explanations   37

	Figs	Page
The trance dance	14–19	38
Metaphors of trance	20–24	50
Stages of trance	25–29	60
Trance experience	30–41	68
Rain-making	42–45	92
Control of animals	46–47	100
The human figure	48–51	104
Equipment	52–54	112
Animals	55–67	118
Other peoples	68–71	142
Complex panels	72–76	148

PART III
Artistic splendour   *165*

PART IV
Viewing the art   *181*
How to view the art   *182*
Where to view the art   *184*
Sites open to the public   *184*
Museums with rock art collections   *188*
Suggestions for further reading   *189*
Some other works cited in this book   *190*
Index   *192*

PART I

The Bushmen and their art

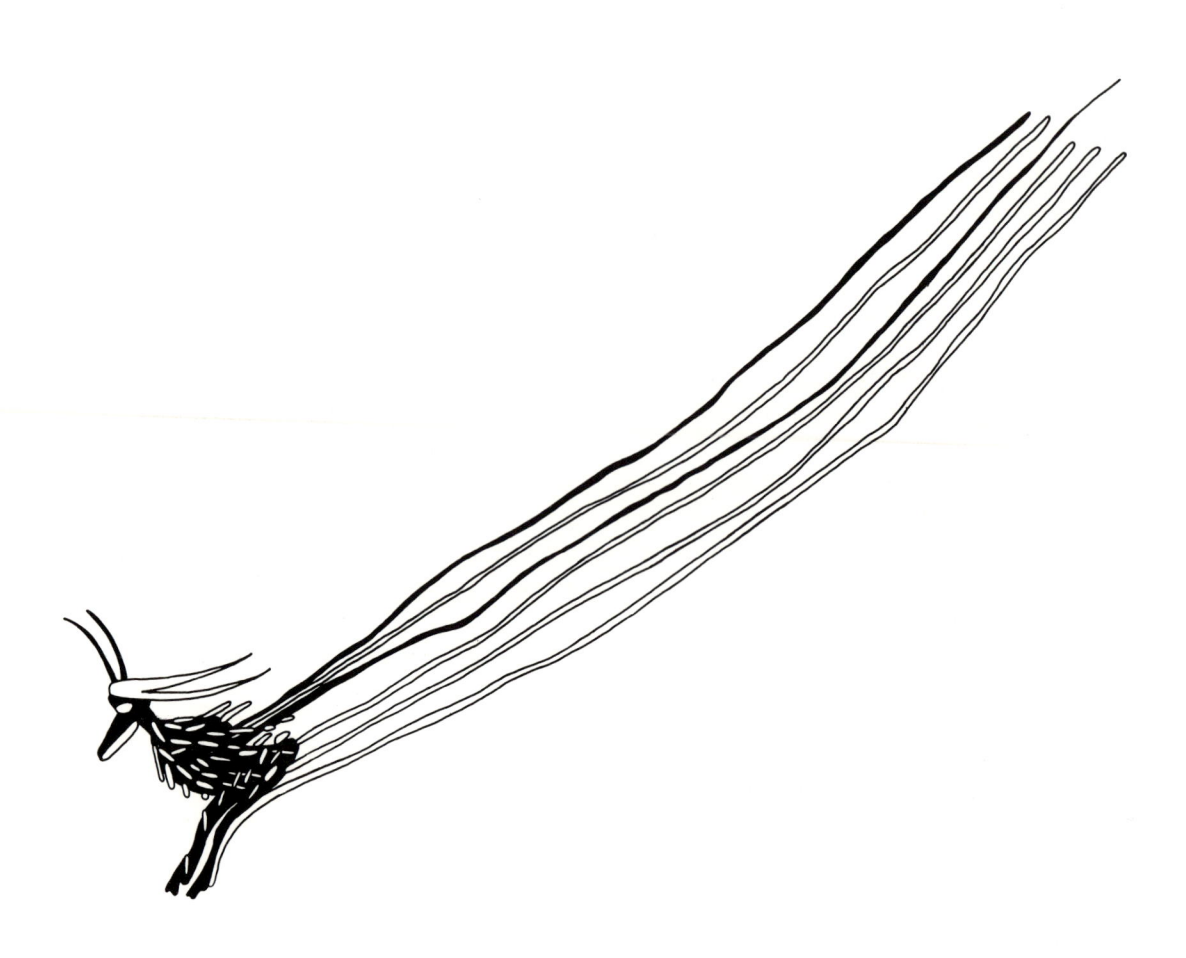

1   Mlambonja rock painting,
    Natal Drakensberg.

2

High above the Mlambonja River, a great boulder stands at the forefront of the Drakensberg ramparts. Resting in the lee of this rock, the climber commands a wide view over Natal: everything falls sharply away until, far in the distance, the sky meets the horizon. Breathtaking as this prospect may be, a more intriguing panorama is at one's back, for on this boulder are some of the world's most interesting rock paintings. One of them is shown on this page. It has both animal and imaginary features and long, trailing streamers. Baffling questions crowd in. Does it depict a mythological personage? A whimsical artist's fancy? A vision? A supernatural being? Or, perhaps, a spirit of the dead?

This book answers these and many other questions about southern African rock art by describing the beliefs and experiences the artists depicted and by drawing attention to usually overlooked details. The best way to use the book is to read it first from beginning to end. Part I gives essential background information and discusses the artists, their way of life and beliefs. It also describes how the rock art was made and how old it is.

Part II then focuses on key features of the art. It has been written so that the explanations of selected paintings follow on one another and lead the reader deeper and deeper into the strange and mysterious world of the ancient artists. Many of these explanations are given in the Bushmen's own words as they were recorded over a century ago.

Part III presents full colour photographs of Bushman rock art. Although these photographs do not show the fine detail as clearly as the copies in Part II, they give a good general idea of the artistic splendour as it is today.

Part IV introduces the practical application of the information given in the first two parts. Take the book to one of the rock art sites or museums listed and, using the index, look up the various subjects depicted. The numbers in brackets on the explanatory pages in Part II are a guide to further helpful sections. You will thus be able to see how each site contains a unique combination of themes.

Mysterious paintings, like the one above the Mlambonja River, will be more – though not entirely – comprehensible; apparently trivial 'scenes of daily life' will take on new and quite different meanings; even the beautiful depictions of animals will yield up layers of significance inaccessible without some glimpse into the minds of the artists.

WHO WERE THE ARTISTS?

In the past there was heated controversy over the identity of the artists. Often it was claimed that exotic peoples made the art. This claim was based on two serious misconceptions that still appear in popular books and, more unfortunately, in some school textbooks. The first misconception concerns the Bushmen themselves, and the second is about specific paintings.

In the first place, many people believe that the Bushmen were too 'primitive' to have been capable of producing such sensitive art. This opinion goes back to the first contact between white colonists and the Bushmen. In 1655 Jan Wintervogel, an ensign sent on an exploratory tour by Van Riebeeck, was travelling to the north of Cape Town in the vicinity of present-day Malmesbury. There he met a group of people whom he described as 'of a very small stature, subsisting very meagerly, quite wild, without huts, cattle or anything in the world'. Two hundred years later, in 1856, the missionary Henry Tindall, who enjoyed little success in converting the Bushmen to Christianity, despairingly told a Cape Town audience: 'He has no religion, no laws, no government, no recognised authority, no patrimony, no fixed abode . . . a soul, debased, it is true, and completely bound down and clogged by his animal nature.'

Since then many authors have expressed similar racist generalisations. They describe the Bushmen as simple and childlike, delighting in bizarre tales, but incapable of abstract thought, belief or symbolism.

Some writers express the widely held opinion that the Bushmen and their art are both 'childlike'. Even a superficial glance at the illustrations in this book will show that the two types of art have little in common and, when the background and meaning of Bushman art are taken into account, it will be obvious that Bushman art is far from childlike. It is, in fact, highly sophisticated.

Other authors emphasise the Bushmen's closeness to nature and, by simple extension, their closeness to animals. A few even believe that the Bushmen did not distinguish between people and animals. At the end of the last century, the historian George McCall Theal summed up these ideas when he wrote that the Bushmen 'were of no benefit to any other section of the human family, they were incapable of improvement, and as it was impossible for civilised men to live on the same soil with them, it was for the world's good that they should make room for a higher race'.

These views are not only repugnant; they are also blatantly wrong. The Bushmen are as intelligent and sensitive as any other human group. Their beliefs are as complex and subtle as those of people who live in what we may consider more complex societies. They are in no way inferior to or different from any other human beings.

'The White Lady of the Brandberg'
(copy by H. Pager).

The second misconception is that the art depicts exotic 'foreigners'. People who believe the Bushmen to be mentally incapable of producing art, naturally have to find alternative artists to account for the immense quantity of rock art in southern Africa, and they seek evidence in the art itself. One of the most influential figures in the study of prehistoric art in Europe and elsewhere, the Abbé Henri Breuil, was responsible for some gross errors that are still encountered today. He believed that he could identify depictions of Minoans, Phoenicians and other Mediterranean people in southern African rock art. The painting that gave rise to his most spectacular blunder, the so-called White Lady of the Brandberg (2), has become a persistent legend, even enjoying the doubtful distinction of appearing in one of Erich von Daniken's books where the author implies that it depicts a being from outer space – the ultimate in exoticism. The story of its discovery and fame is particularly relevant because it illustrates some disastrous trends that have damaged rock art research and discredited it in the eyes of professional archaeologists and other interested people.

The painting was discovered in 1917 by Reinhardt Maack, who was preparing a map of the Brandberg, the famous mountain in Namibia. While on a visit to South Africa in 1929, Breuil saw Maack's copy of the painting but did not visit the site. When the Abbé returned to South Africa during the Second World War, he was able to examine more recent photographs of the painting and, fired with new enthusiasm, he wrote to General J.C. Smuts, who was then prime minister:

I send you the portrait of a charming girl, who has been waiting for us on a rock in the Brandberg range for perhaps three thousand years; do you think it well to keep her waiting much longer?

Although Smuts did not grant Breuil's request for transport to the Brandberg, the Abbé knew he was assured of a sympathetic hearing. Smuts, who, like many others at that time, considered the Bushman 'mentally stunted' and 'a desert animal', could be expected to welcome the discovery of any evidence of European influence in the art.

Eventually, in 1947, when Breuil did manage to reach the remote Brandberg, he continued his romanticising:

As we approached the place, the impression it conveyed of a great fallen acropolis or palace was intensified; between the granite slabs and boulders there are flat sand-covered surfaces like squares or courts between dwellings. At noon on the day of our arrival in the ravine, we climbed a natural stairway and passed two boulders. We then found ourselves confronting the painting which had been haunting me for eighteen years and which we had come so far to see.

Throughout his description of the site and its environs, Breuil conjures up a picture of a ruined Minoan or Greek city, despite the fact that the place is a perfectly natural, arid mountain valley. He thus cleverly sets the scene for the 'discovery' to come.

In such surroundings, the reader is led to believe, one would not be surprised to find something exotic, startling and strange. Indeed, many rock art books, following Breuil's lead, seem more concerned with spectacular scenery, the hardships endured getting to remote sites and the thrill of discovery than with the paintings themselves.

While copying the paintings, Breuil was visited by Colonel Hoogenhout, the Administrator of the territory, who declared, apparently with Breuil's approval, 'This is no Bushman painting: this is Great Art!' When Smuts saw Breuil's copy, he was even more effusive. According to Breuil, he exclaimed, 'You have upset all my history ... When you publish these paintings, you will set the world on fire and nobody will believe you.' The legend of the White Lady of the Brandberg was well and truly launched.

More recent and sober research has questioned Breuil's interpretation. In the first place, the White Lady is a male figure, a point on which Maack had no doubt. As Harald Pager's meticulous copy shows, close inspection reveals it has a penis. It also carries a bow and arrows, specifically male equipment. Certainly, the White Lady lacks the Mediterranean profile that Breuil claimed for it, and the fact that the lower half of the figure is painted in white in no way implies that it depicts a European. The Bushmen did not always use colours realistically. Elephants, for instance, were painted in red, black or white. In any event, white human figures abound in Bushman rock art and most of them are clearly Bushmen. Finally, and perhaps most importantly, just above the White Lady there is an antelope with human hindlegs, and this alone argues against a rigorously literal interpretation of the panel.

The White Lady and accompanying figures are clearly Bushman rock paintings, striking but no different from many paintings throughout southern Africa. Only someone unfamiliar with the broad sweep of Bushman rock art would wish to single out the White Lady for special treatment.

Another myth about southern African rock art must be consigned to oblivion: the famous White Lady of the Brandberg is neither white nor a lady.

But, at the time, Breuil was greatly encouraged by the enthusiastic reception of his views on ancient Mediterranean influences in southern Africa, and he went on to 'discover' paintings of Phoenicians in the Natal Drakensberg (72).

Less improbable artists have also been suggested. For instance, a persuasive case has been made for Khoikhoi ('Hottentot') authorship of paintings in the southwestern Cape. There seems to be some correlation between certain kinds of painting, especially handprints (50), and the areas occupied by the Khoikhoi, who moved into the southwestern Cape about 1500 years ago. Unlike Bushmen, they had flocks of sheep and, in more recent times, herds of cattle. However, even if the Khoikhoi did paint some of the art, most of the paintings in the region seem to reflect Bushman beliefs. Iron Age black farming people (69) have also made some rock art. It is generally done in thick white or red paint and often depicts geometric forms. Some rock engravings believed to have been made by black farmers seem to be 'plans' of stone-walled Iron Age settlements. Iron Age rock art is therefore easily distinguished from Bushman rock art.

Whatever the contributions of the Khoikhoi and black farmers to southern African rock art may have been, the early white settlers accepted that the Bushmen had made the art in the rock shelters, even though some were surprised by this evidence of sensitivity. Those few Bushmen who were interviewed on the subject or to whom copies were shown accepted that the art had been made by their own people. For instance, in the 1870s, George William Stow showed some copies he had made of rock paintings to an old Bushman couple. On seeing a depiction of a dance, the old woman began to sing and dance. Her husband was so moved by the memories she awakened that he begged her to stop. 'Don't,' he said, 'don't sing those old songs, I can't bear it! It makes my heart too sad!' She persisted, however; finally, the old man joined her. They looked at each other, Stow wrote, and were happy, the glance of the wife seeming to say, 'Ah! I thought you could not withstand *that*!'

All the extravagant ideas about foreigners are now no more than an amusing footnote: today no professional archaeologist doubts that the vast bulk of southern African rock art was made by the Bushmen.

THE BUSHMEN

The Bushmen belong to the so-called Khoisan group of people, which comprises the Khoikhoi (or Khoekhoe) and the San or Bushmen. There is no single word used by all Bushmen to designate themselves; each group has its own word. For instance, a group in northern Namibia and Botswana, commonly called !Kung by anthropologists, refer to themselves as Zu/'hoasi, which means 'completed people'. The word 'Bushmen', a translation of the Dutch *Boschjesmans*, was applied in the seventeenth century to all the groups. It is now felt that, for some people, 'Bushmen' has become an insulting word associated with the old, racist views we have already mentioned and dismissed. It is certainly true that words like 'Bushmen' are often used to lump together various distinct groups so that they can be easily manipulated by those in power. Even today some people with political power argue, quite incorrectly, that 'Bushmen' have no rights to their own land because they were nomadic 'people of the bush'. As the rock art shows, Bushmen lived in all parts of southern Africa.

'San', the word the Nama Khoikhoi people used for all Bushman groups, is today preferred by many anthropologists, and the Bushmen are known by this name in academic journals and books. Unfortunately, 'San' also has highly pejorative associations. The Nama applied it not just to the original hunters of the subcontinent but to any impoverished, cattleless people; in fact, as Mathias Guenther puts it, it was applied to 'the flotsam and jetsam of the pluralist society of the Cape'. It seems unfair to the 150 000 modern Nama speakers to take one of their terms of opprobrium and to apply it to the Bushmen, even though its pejorative associations are not keenly felt outside Nama society. There seems to be no easy way out of the difficulty of what word to use. In this book we have decided to retain the better-known term 'Bushmen', but, as should be clear, we use it without insulting overtones.

The Bushmen have always been considered a somewhat mysterious people. At one time it was fashionable to link them to Asian populations or even to the lost tribes of Israel, but modern research has shown that they are unquestionably African in origin.

Skeletal remains of Bushman type can be traced back to the Later Stone Age, or to about 10 000 years ago. These very early proto-Bushman people were descended from much earlier African populations represented by such skulls as those found at Hopefield in the Cape, Florisbad in the Orange Free State, and Kabwe in Zambia.

Studies of the genetic characteristics of the Bushmen and the Negroid people suggest that they have much in common. The divergence between them probably accelerated when the Negroid people, who speak Bantu languages and were living farther to the north, later took to agriculture, and the Khoisan remained what anthropologists call foragers or hunter-gatherers. Still later, the Khoikhoi acquired flocks and herds and became distinguishable from the Bushmen, though not nearly as markedly as was

Kalahari !Kung Bushman bowman
(photo: L. Marshall). 3

formerly supposed. Then, especially in the nineteenth century, the divergence began to close as Bushmen and Negroid people started to intermarry again.

Today, remnants of the Bushmen survive only in the Kalahari Desert. Contrary to popular belief, these survivors are not descendants of the southern painters who were driven into inhospitable areas by more powerful peoples; they make no rock art and have no tradition of rock art. Some of them are aware of paintings in the Tsodilo hills, but, as Megan Biesele found, they say god put them there. The groups who lived farther to the south and made the art spoke different languages. They became extinct about a century ago as a result of white colonisation (70-71).

The principal Bushman groups are not political entities, like tribes, but linguistic divisions. The Bushmen and the Khoikhoi speak phonetically very complex 'click' languages. The different clicks are represented by !, /, //, and ≠. Some Bantu languages have, through prolonged and close contact with Bushmen, adopted some of their clicks. In these Bantu languages the clicks are represented by letters of the alphabet: q, c and x. There are a great many Bushman language groups, such as the !Kung of the northern Kalahari, the !Kõ of the central Kalahari, and the now-extinct /Xam of the Cape south of the Orange River. Even though many of these languages are mutually unintelligible, the way of life practised by the various groups is – or was – broadly similar.

WAY OF LIFE

In earlier times, all these Bushman groups were hunter-gatherers. The men hunted game and other animals, whereas the women gathered plant foods. To modern Westerners this may seem a precarious way of living, but their life was not one of unremitting labour, eking out a miserable, sordid and anxious existence. Even in the more arid areas of southern Africa, there was plenty of time for talking, visiting, making beadwork, and other activities, though there were, of course, times of drought and hardship. But even in extended droughts, hunter-gatherers are better off than farmers because they can exploit a variety of hardy natural foods and can move to better-watered regions.

Because the Bushmen lived entirely off the land, they had to be nomadic. It was not long before the women had to walk excessive distances to gather food. Bushman groups did not, however, wander aimlessly or relentlessly pursue herds of antelope. Instead, they followed a carefully planned annual route that took them to different areas of plant food as, season by season, these foods ripened. In some regions, like the Natal Drakensberg, migratory game followed the same annual round as the Bushmen, but in other regions the people waited for summer rain storms and the animals attracted by them. As a nineteenth century Bushman put it, 'The bushes will sprout and become nicely green, so that the springbok come galloping.'

These yearly cycles must have had great meaning for the Bushmen and probably provided the same sense of security that a fixed abode affords other people. The Bushmen's attachment to certain places is evident in a sad account of their last decades in the eastern Cape. George William Stow described how a small family group persisted in moving from rock shelter to rock shelter despite the threat posed by the white farmers, who were determined to exterminate them.

These mobile groups comprised up to about 25 men, women and children. At certain times of the year a number of groups amalgamated, although this may not have been a universal feature of Bushman life. These times provided an opportunity for the exchange of news and gifts, for marriage arrangements and for pleasant social occasions. But at all times people moved between camps so that the membership of a group was not static for a long period. Moving off to join relatives in another camp was one of the ways of dealing with social tension. People were free to come and go as they pleased, and everyone maintained contacts with a number of groups as a kind of insurance policy.

This constant exchange of membership was made possible by the generally egalitarian nature of Bushman society. Bushmen have no chiefs or ruling elite. Indeed, the southern /Xam language had no word for chief. In the Kalahari, certain individuals may assume leadership in specific spheres in which they excel, such as hunting or ritual curing, but they cannot achieve positions of general influence or power. Important decisions that affect the group as a whole are discussed by everyone – men and women – until consensus is reached. The early white colonists found this egalitarianism and mobility confusing when they tried to establish treaties with Bushmen. On the Bushman side, contact with the settlers seems to have led to certain people being accepted as spokesmen, but it is not clear what more general status they held among their people. Today, with many Bushmen settled on white-owned farms, ritual curers are becoming more prominent.

Egalitarianism and changing membership of groups, even across linguistic boundaries, led to widespread uniformity of Bushman life and belief. This is not to say that all Bushman groups were identical, certainly there were regional differences, but research has shown that the fundamentals of Bushman social organisation and religion were, to all intents and purposes, universal.

BUSHMAN RELIGION

The most important southern Bushman spiritual being was /Kaggen, the trickster-deity. He created all things, and he appears in numerous myths where he can be foolish or wise, tiresome or helpful. Often other characters lecture him on how one should behave.

The word '/Kaggen' can be translated as 'mantis', and this led to the belief that the Bushmen 'worshipped' the praying mantis. This insect is still sometimes (and insultingly) referred to as the 'Hottentotsgod' or, worse, 'hotnotsgod'. However, /Kaggen neither *is* nor *is not* a praying mantis: the mantis is only one of his many manifestations. He can also turn into a bull eland, a hare, a louse, a snake or a vulture; he can assume many forms.

In a remarkably apt statement, a nineteenth century Bushman described /Kaggen's ability to assume these different forms. It appears that, on Guy Fawkes day 1874, some white children had put on masks and had attempted to frighten and tease some Bushmen. This incident struck one of the men as illustrative of /Kaggen's nature:

> */Kaggen imitates what people do when they want us who do not know Guy Fawkes to be afraid. They change their faces, for they want us who do not know to think that it is not a person.*

When he is not in one of his animal manifestations, /Kaggen lives the life of an ordinary Bushman, hunting, fighting and getting into scrapes. Many tales tell of his conflicts with various people and his escapes. As we shall see, the way in which he escapes is relevant to Bushman rock art (22).

The modern !Kung of the Kalahari, along with other Bushman groups, believe in two gods: one who lives in the east and one who lives in the west. Like the southern Bushmen, they believe in spirits of the dead, but not as part of ancestor worship. The spirits are generally only vaguely identified and are thought to bring sickness and death. So-called 'medicine people' protect everyone from the spirits and sickness. This is done at a 'medicine dance', a ritual we describe in detail in a later section (14-19).

For the Bushmen, religion is not a separate part of life to be indulged in only on certain solemn and ritual occasions. It is part of the fabric of everyday existence: no clear distinction is drawn between sacred and secular. This is one of the reasons why their beliefs about and attitude towards the supernatural are important for a proper understanding of their art.

DISTRIBUTION OF BUSHMAN ROCK ART

The mysterious Mlambonja creature is *painted* on a Drakensberg boulder.

Elsewhere in southern Africa, depictions are *engraved* on rocks. Paintings and engravings are, by and large, found in different parts of southern Africa (4).

Rock paintings occur principally, but not exclusively, in mountainous regions where there are abundant rock shelters. Major ranges such as the Drakensberg, the Malutis, the Brandberg, the Cedarberg and the Waterberg have a great many paintings (5). In other areas, isolated koppies with shallow overhangs may also have paintings. The southern part of the Kruger National Park is rich in this kind of site. Sometimes hillside boulders, like the Mlambonja rock, have overhangs beneath which there are paintings. In some areas of the subcontinent, such as the Drakensberg, virtually every inhabitable rock shelter has paintings or the remains of paintings. The pioneering southern African archaeologist, 'Peter' van Riet Lowe, called this region 'the richest storehouse of prehistoric art in the world'. This is not an extravagant claim.

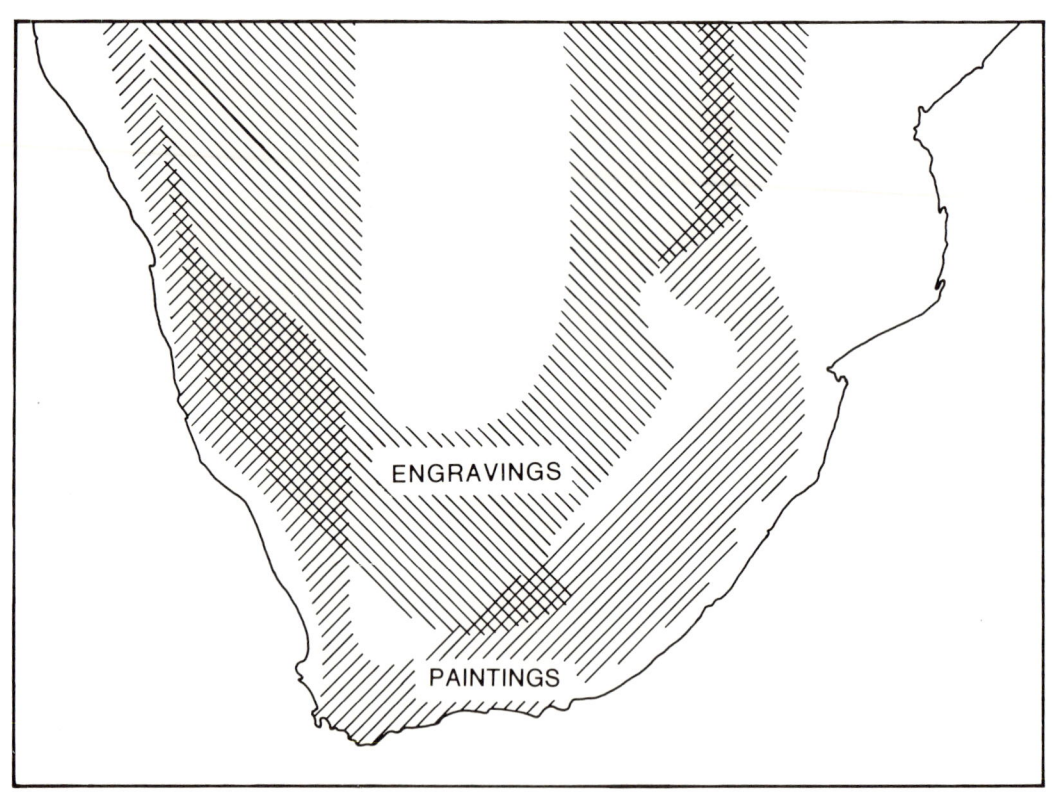

Map showing painted and engraved regions of southern Africa (after C. van Riet Lowe, 1941).

All southern African rock paintings were done in open rock shelters, not in dark subterranean caverns. Contrary to popular opinion, elevated sites, like the one overlooking the Mlambonja Valley, were not necessarily chosen for defence or for the extensive views they afford; there are also many painted shelters tucked away in narrow valleys. It would, in any event, be far more prudent for a band of hunter-gatherers to flee than to risk being besieged in a rock shelter.

Because rock shelters are frequently quite shallow, paintings are often exposed to rain, and this has contributed to their poor preservation. Painted sites that afford little or no shelter present intriguing problems. Did the people live in nearby temporary grass huts or did they journey to these sites solely to make or to look at the paintings? We do not yet know the answer to these questions. Moreover, some rock shelters are so densely painted that one cannot help wondering if they acquired some special significance beyond the mundane considerations of shelter, warmth and proximity to water. The

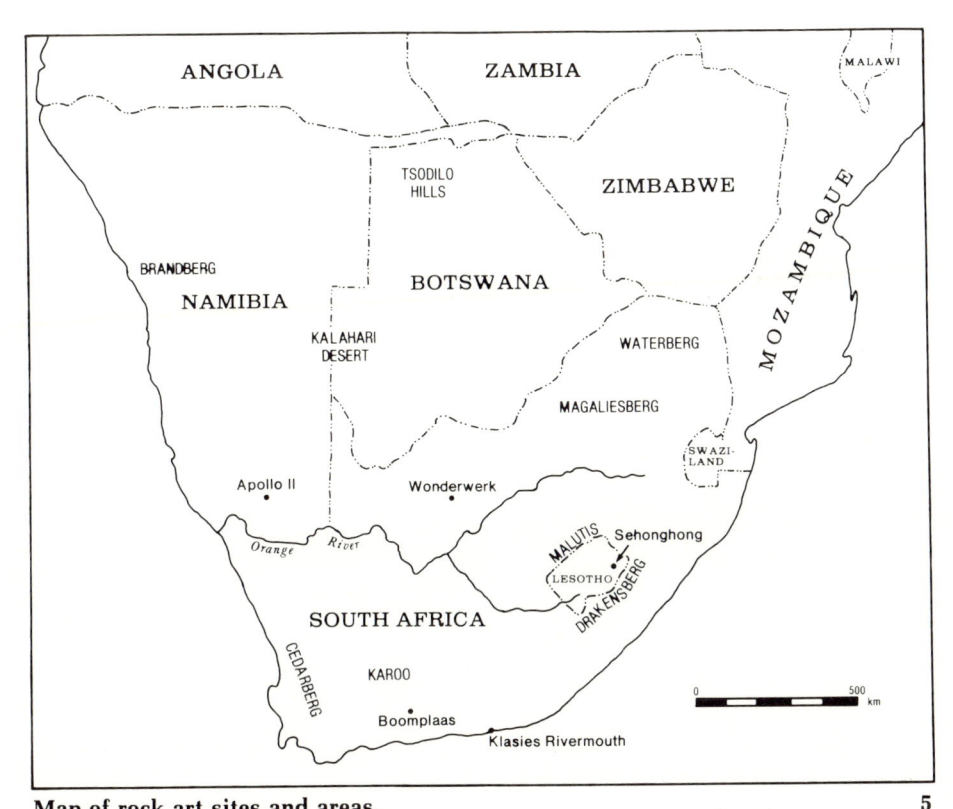

Map of rock art sites and areas. 5

explanations in Part II suggest that some painted rock shelters may well have been considered particularly powerful places.

In contrast to the paintings, rock engravings are found principally on the interior plateau; for example, in the vicinity of Kimberley, the Magaliesberg and the Karoo. Low rises with a scatter of exposed rocks are typical engraving sites (7). The rocks offer no shelter, and the people probably lived in dwellings made of grass and branches, as do the modern Kalahari Bushmen.

Various attempts have been made to divide southern Africa into rock art regions. All these studies start with the different distributions of paintings and engravings that we have noted and then move on to distinguish between different painted areas. For instance, the paintings in the western Cape seem to be stiffer and to show less animation than the Drakensberg ones. They also seem to be predominantly painted in one colour (monochrome), usually red, whereas the Drakensberg paintings are more

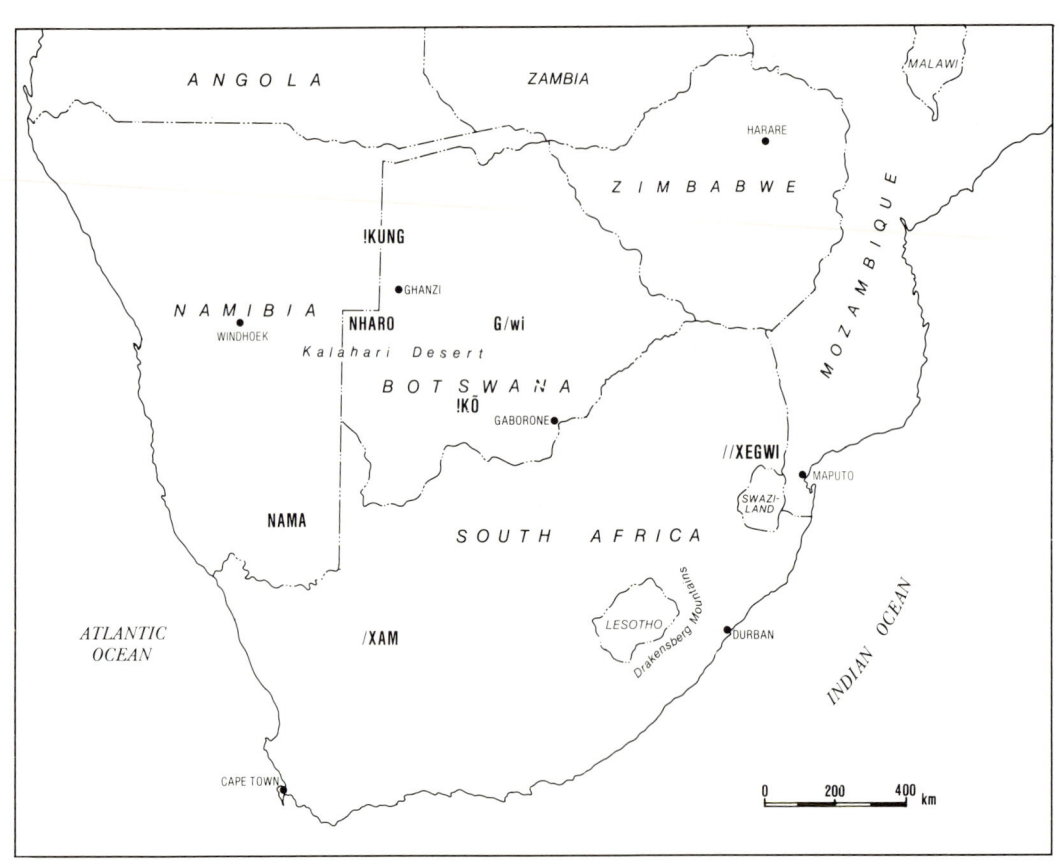

Map of Bushman groups.

A rock engraving site.

frequently done in two (bichrome) or more colours (polychrome). This particular distinction may, however, be largely illusory. Black and white paints are more fugitive than red. If the western Cape paintings are somewhat older than many of those in the Drakensberg, as they may well be, we should expect to find a predominance of red monochrome paintings, the black and white paint having disappeared. On the other hand, it does seem that the well-known shaded polychrome paintings (55-59) are an almost exclusive feature of the Drakensberg-Maluti region.

Farther to the north, the art of Namibia appears to have more in common with that in Zimbabwe than with the western Cape art. The northern Transvaal art, too, seems to belong to the Namibia-Zimbabwe group. The paintings in this vast northern region are very diverse, and the emphasis on eland that characterises the art of the western Cape and the Drakensberg is absent. Other animals such as kudu are prominent. None the less, as in other regions, there are many polychrome paintings, though, with perhaps one exception, no shaded polychromes.

These regions are still only vaguely defined, and we do not know what they mean. Do they, for instance, reflect linguistic divisions? Or are they simply the result of such 'stylistic' differences as one may expect over such a vast region?

In any event, regions defined simply by look-alike qualities are unsatisfactory. It would be better to select clearly defined and unmistakable criteria of known meaning and to use these to establish regions. But then further problems arise. What criteria should we choose? If, for example, we decided on a certain proportion of eland to depictions of other antelope, we should arrive at regions different from those that would be established by using the proportion of animal to human depictions as a criterion. Both of these regional patterns would cut across the well-accepted painting and engraving regions. This point shows that rock art regions are not 'given'; they are created by researchers. Moreover, without a clear idea of the purpose for which the regions are being established and the significance of the criteria selected, the whole enterprise is meaningless. One cannot divide up the subcontinent according to blindly selected criteria of unknown significance and then try to work out what the resulting regions signify. If the selected criteria are in fact meaningless and trivial, the regions too will be meaningless.

A great deal more research is required to resolve this problem. Until this work is done, we can accept that the art over the whole of southern Africa has much in common, while not allowing this uniformity to obscure the differences that do exist.

TECHNIQUE

Paintings

The Mlambonja creature was painted in red and white. The red pigment used by the rock artists was principally ochre or ferric oxide ground down to a fine powder. Various shades of red and burnt sienna can be obtained by heating ferric oxide in a fire. Red is the most durable colour. White, usually a more fugitive colour, was made from a range of substances, including silica, clay and gypsum. Black paint was made from charcoal, soot and minerals such as manganese.

The use of different pigments is spoken of in a story told by a /Xam Bushman in the 1870s. In this tale a girl says, 'It is //*hara*, therefore I think I shall draw a gemsbok with it.' Her companion replies, 'It is *tó*, therefore I think I shall draw a springbok with it.' //*Hara* is black specularite, and *tó* is red haematite. This story does not, however, mean that all springbok and gemsbok are painted in those two colours. It simply shows that the narrator not only knew about rock paintings, but that he even knew some of the ingredients for different paints.

The medium, or liquid, in which these pigments were mixed has been the subject of much controversy. Generally, paintings are so weathered that only the pigment remains, but chemical tests done on some thicker paints have revealed the presence of amino acids. Blood was the probable source of these amino acids, and the use of antelope blood in the manufacture of paint was recorded by some early writers. Other possible media that have been suggested include fat, urine, eggwhite and plant sap. A good deal of research remains to be done on the ingredients of the paint, but researchers are reluctant to undertake the work because it inevitably entails the destruction or partial destruction of paintings and, if good samples are required, of the best-preserved and most striking paintings.

In some instances the paint was applied to the rock with a finger, but the extraordinary fine lines of so many of the paintings suggest the use of quills, feathers or very thin bones. Mapote, an old man who painted in 1930 for Marion How, wife of the magistrate at Qachasnek, fixed feathers on the ends of tiny reeds.

Mapote provided a valuable demonstration of how the Lesotho Bushmen painted. Although he was himself of Sotho and Pondomise descent, he had half-Bushman stepbrothers and had learned to paint with Bushmen in their caves. Sadly, he told Marion How that he had thought he would ask a friend to join him as he tried to revive his old skill, but he could think of no one: 'They are all dead that I could ask.'

Mapote took some trouble in selecting a suitable stone on which to paint. It had to be smooth and, at the same time, porous enough to absorb the paint. In the end he chose a smooth sandstone. For red pigment he desired what he called *qhang qhang*, a glistening haematite dug out of the basalt mountains. It had to be prepared at full moon out of doors by a woman who heated it over a fire until it was red hot. After this treatment, the pigment was ground between two stones to a fine powder. Mapote then announced that he needed 'the blood of a freshly killed eland', but, no eland being available, he had to mix his paint with ox blood. For white paint he used a white clay and the juice of the plant *Asclepia gibba* (milk weed). His black paint was made from charcoal and water. Using a different brush for each colour, he commenced painting an eland. He started at the animal's chest and moved his brush along smoothly without the slightest hesitation. As Marion How watched, the ancient and long-dead art of rock painting came alive, and lived for a fleeting hour or two. Then, his painting completed and having been rewarded with a new pair of boots, Mapote set off on his long journey home and disappeared into the vast valleys and ranges of the Malutis.

Engravings

No comparable demonstration of how rock engravings were made was ever obtained. The engravings themselves, however, show that they were made by three techniques: pecking, incising and scraping.

Pecked engravings were made by hammering the surface of a rock so that the dark outer skin, or patina, was removed and the lighter interior rock showed through. Some pecked engravings of the so-called 'classic style' are very finely done: they show folds of skin and detail such as antelope ears and eyes, and a zebra's stripes. Because great accuracy must have been required to make these engravings, it seems probable that the artists used a stone punch and hammer. The punch could then be carefully placed before the blow was struck.

In contrast to pecked engravings, *incised engravings* were made by cutting through the patina with another stone. Some engravings are quite deeply incised, but other fine-line engravings are very shallow. The instrument could have been a piece of the same stone, because the patina through which the cut was made is softer than the interior, unweathered stone; there is no need to propose the use of diamonds as some writers have done. With the passage of time the patina forms again, and the engravings may be difficult to see.

Scraped engravings, as the name suggests, were made by scraping away the patina or part of the patina. Generally, they seem to be more recent than pecked or incised engravings and, at any rate to the Western eye, they are not as beautiful, though many of them are of great interest.

Learning the techniques

How did the artists learn these painting and engraving techniques? Where did they practise? Most of the art seems highly accomplished, and one seldom, if ever, encounters what appear to be preliminary sketches or the attempts of novices. One possibility is that learners practised on some perishable material, like hide, that has not survived. Another suggestion is that they practised by drawing in the sand. This, however, seems unlikely because sand drawings would not prepare an artist for the extraordinarily fine lines, delicate shading and tiny details the paintings in particular display.

The most probable explanation is that novices learned by apprenticing themselves to an experienced artist and acquired the necessary skills by actually participating in the production of pictures. Having done an outline, a painter may have requested his student to fill in the colour; or, having done one ear of an antelope, he may have told the student to do the other. Learning by participating rather than by formal instruction is how Bushmen acquired many other skills.

THE AGE OF THE ART

As Marion How's experience with Mapote and other reports show, the most recent paintings were done in the 1880s and 1890s, and perhaps even more recently by the few Bushmen who survived in the Drakensberg and Maluti mountains. Some of these paintings are easily dated because they depict white settlers and their horses (70, 71). The other end of the time scale is more difficult to define.

At present it is virtually impossible to date rock paintings by radiocarbon, the way organic finds are usually dated, but important work is being done on particles of carbon present in some black paints. These particles are so minute that an atomic accelerator has to be used to measure the amount of radioactive carbon present. Working with this sort of paint sample from the western Cape, Nick van der Merwe and his fellow researchers obtained a date of approximately 500 B.P. (years before the present) for paint taken from a human figure that appears to have been drawn with a finger dipped in black paint.

Until this dating technique has been more extensively applied, we shall have to rely on painted and engraved stones retrieved from deposits in cave sites. These stones vary from about the size of a hand to about 30 cm across. Some were placed in graves, but most were simply part of the accumulation of cave debris. Although neither the stone itself nor the paint on it can be dated, carbon from the stratum in which they were found can be used.

Dates thus obtained show that painted mobile art, as these stones are called, was being made as long ago as 26 300 (± 400) B.P. This astonishingly early date comes from Eric Wendt's excavation in the Apollo 11 shelter in southern Namibia (8). It means that at least some southern African rock art was contemporaneous with the Upper Palaeolithic art of Western Europe. The most famous of the European painted caves, Lascaux, has been dated to about 17 000 B.P., ten thousand years later than the Apollo 11 art.

The great age of the Apollo 11 mobile art counts against the belief that the practice of painting on rocks spread by diffusion from Europe, through East Africa to southern Africa. Southern African rock art is more probably an independent tradition, and today archaeologists believe that there is little or no evidence for the diffusionist explanation. Other painted stones, notably from Hilary and Janette Deacon's excavation at Boomplaas, near Oudtshoorn, have been dated to 6 400 B.P. and 2000 B.P. Still others, from Ronald Singer and John Wymer's excavation at Klasies River Mouth, have been dated to 2 285 and 4 110 B.P. The Deacons are now continuing the Klasies River Mouth excavations, and more rock art may be found and dated.

The paintings on the Apollo 11, Oudtshoorn and Klasies River stones show animals and geometric forms.

One of the Apollo 11 stones bears a depiction of what appears to be a feline, but it has human hindlegs that may have been added after the completion of the animal (8). Significantly, one of the Apollo 11 animals has been painted in two colours. This calls in question the commonly held belief that the oldest art is monochrome and that bichrome and polychrome paintings are much later developments. It seems more likely that people used more than one colour from very early times. These discoveries also suggest that the whole question of the evolution of rock art styles needs to be re-examined. 'Styles', once the rock art researcher's principal interest, are very difficult to define objectively, and none of the suggested sequences has been generally accepted.

Rock engraving also seems to be a technique of considerable antiquity. Securely dated mobile art from Anne and Francis Thackeray's excavation in Wonderwerk Cave near Kimberley shows that people were engraving over 10 000 years ago. One of these stones bears an unfinished mammal, another the hindquarters of a zebra, while others have grid patterns (9).

Attempts have also been made to date the rock engravings of the open sites by geomorphological techniques. This research suggests dates ranging between 3000 and 4000 years. A new technique, cation-ratio dating, developed by Ronald Dorn and David Whitley, uses small quantities of the so-called desert varnish that accumulates on rocks in arid and semi-arid areas. The results of this technique are still awaited.

In any event, we may be confident that rock engraving and painting were practised in southern Africa for many thousands of years. It is,

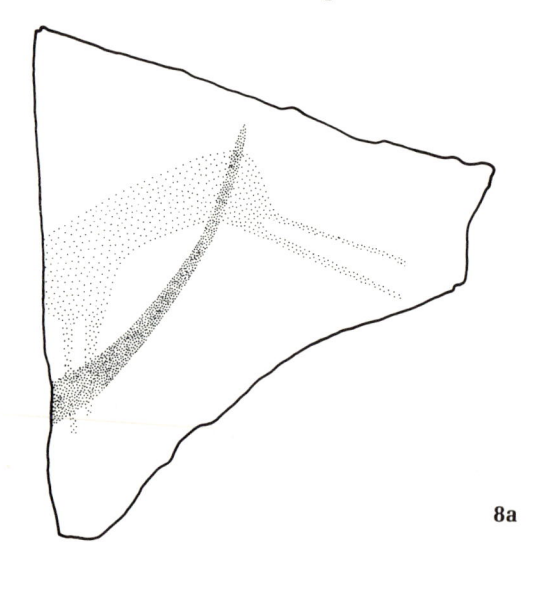

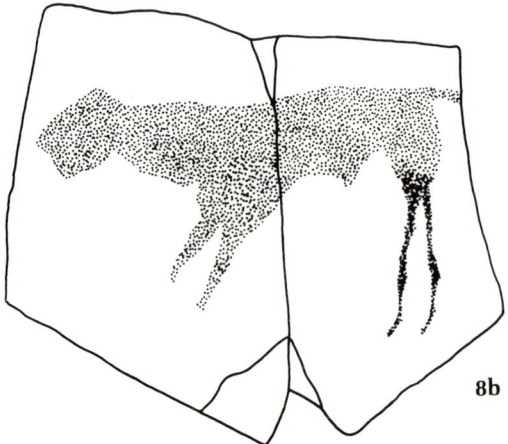

8a

8b

Two painted stones from the Apollo 11 shelter, southern Namibia (after E. Wendt).

9a

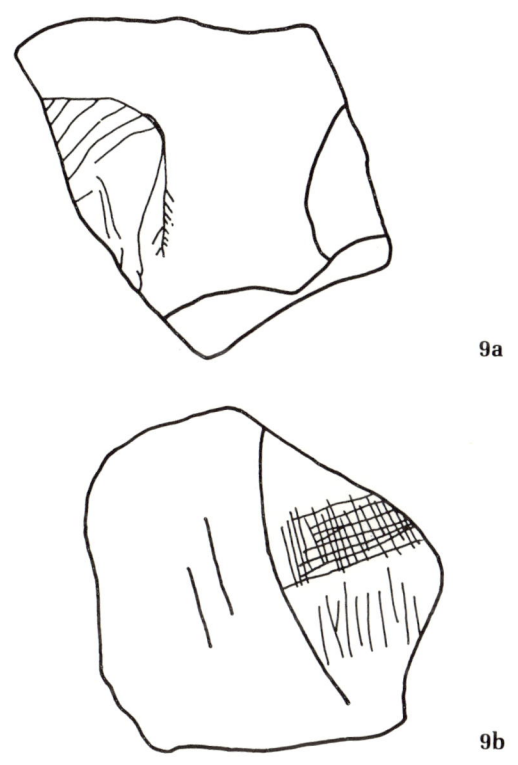

9b

Two engraved stones from the Wonderwerk Cave, northern Cape (after Thackery et al.).

however, unlikely that any of the paintings preserved in the rock shelters are of such great antiquity because cave walls crumble and flake at a faster rate. Just how old they are we do not know. Nor do we know how old most of the rock engravings on the hilltops are; because of their more durable nature, they may be much older than paintings in rock shelters.

Whatever the case, the art we see today in southern Africa represents the longest artistic tradition human beings have produced. As we shall see, it was the persistence of this Stone Age tradition into historical times that provides an unusually promising opportunity for understanding rock art. Indeed, some curious depictions, like the one on the Mlambonja rock, probably represent concepts that originated deep in the human past.

WHAT DOES THE ART MEAN?

Older interpretations

Mistaken ideas about the mental capabilities of so-called 'primitive people' and a lack of close attention to the art itself are the basic ingredients of a recipe for misunderstanding. It was, in fact, this combination that led to one of the earliest interpretations of Bushman rock art – sympathetic magic.

The sympathetic-magic explanation proposes that people made depictions of animals prior to a hunt in the belief that the act of depiction or of shooting arrows at the depictions would ensure success. At the beginning of this century, sympathetic magic was considered to explain the Upper Palaeolithic art in such European cave sites as Altamira and Font-de-Gaume. Researchers who had spent much of their lives studying the French and Spanish art brought the idea to southern Africa. This explanation was never as widely held in southern Africa as it was in Europe because there is no evidence that the Bushmen believed in sympathetic magic of that kind and because the art seems to be too diverse for so restricted an explanation.

Another explanation has achieved far more acceptance because it seems to accord better with the supposed diversity of the art. It is that the Bushmen painted whatever caught their fancy: hunting escapades, fights, dances, amusing incidents, meat-providing animals, an occasional 'mythical' figure, and so forth.

This view has been put forward in so many popular books and articles that it is deeply ingrained in many people's view of the art. They believe that, because the art is little more than a record of daily life, anyone can look at it and – without any knowledge of the Bushmen, their life and beliefs – tell what the pictures mean. Inevitably, the art is reduced to amusing vignettes and becomes a vehicle for a writer's ingenuity and a target for his jibes and drollery. At its worst this kind of writing is exemplified by claims for the detection of fur-lined leggings, drunken brawls, 'singularly beautiful home-decorating', humorous caricatures and, in what is probably the most absurd of all comments on rock art anywhere in the world, the use of enemas.

There are numerous reasons why such comments distort Bushman rock art. Perhaps the most telling reason is that they result from viewing the art through Western eyes. Contrary to the adage that every picture tells a story, it is not possible to get at the meaning of a work of art without some guidance from the artist or, at the very least, a thorough understanding of the culture from which it comes.

Take, as a simple example, a well-known statue by Auguste Rodin. It depicts a young man with one hand placed on top of his head and the other held clenched. Without any knowledge of Rodin's intention, one could easily suppose that the statue portrayed grief or youth or, as early critics believed, that it was simply a remarkably lifelike piece lacking further meaning. In fact, Rodin first entitled it *The Vanquished*, but later changed the title to *The Age of Bronze*. Under its second title, the statue has a hand placed on its head because Rodin believed (quite erroneously) that humankind's intellectual capacities emerged during the Bronze Age. The other hand once held a bronze spear because Rodin believed, along with many people of his time, that technological advances freed people and permitted the development of art, philosophy and religion. Later Rodin removed the spear because it obstructed the view of the figure from certain angles.

A Westerner could discover none of this simply by looking at the statue, even though it comes from Western tradition. It is, then, far less likely that a Westerner can look at a foreign art like that of the Bushmen and know intuitively what it means.

Yet this is exactly what the Abbé Breuil thought he could do with his White Lady. Similarly, if the strange Mlambonja creature is seen only from a Western point of view, it remains forever unintelligible. Each art must be seen, as far as it is possible, from the point of view of the people who created it. If we do not try to adopt the artists' viewpoint, we may appreciate and enjoy an exotic art's beauty, but we shall never know what it *means*.

Adopting a foreign perspective is, of course, no easy matter. It is very difficult to think oneself into other people's minds and, inevitably, our response will be inadequate; even though we now know a great deal, we do not respond to all the nuances intended by the creators of Bushman art. Perhaps this is particularly so with depictions of animals. A representation of, for instance, an eland says to us little more than 'This is an eland', and we could easily conclude, as some rock art writers have done, that the artist was merely painting or engraving something he or she saw in the veld and wanted to 're-see' at home.

To appreciate how shallow this response is, consider the four large bronze lions Edwin Landseer made to lie at the foot of Nelson's Column in Trafalgar Square. Do they merely depict four lions such as one may see in a zoo? A moment's reflection tells us there is much more to it than that. Why did Landseer not make four skunks, or four foxes, or four snakes? Clearly, those animals have, for us, the wrong associations. We associate skunks with bad smells, foxes with cunning, and snakes – a more complex symbol – with evil in certain contexts. In other cultures, however, skunks, foxes and snakes may have more positive associations. Indeed, in ancient Egypt the cobra represented the goddess Wadjet, the preserver of royal authority. So it is quite clear that Landseer chose lions because of their associations, for English people, of regality, nobility and strength.

Most animals have specific but different associations for people in different parts of the world. It is impossible to depict an animal without in some way evoking its associations in the minds of the viewers. So too for the Bushmen. Their artists could not depict a lion without referring to at least some of its associations. For Westerners looking at Bushman art and wisely excluding the Trafalgar Square lions, these associations may be no more than 'predator'. But for Bushmen the lion had important religious and ritual meanings which would be impossible to guess at without an understanding of Bushman culture and belief (63). This book differs from many others in that it tries not to confuse Landseer's view of lions with the Bushman view. We are not interested in a Western response to the art. On the contrary, we want to know how the Bushmen responded and what *they* thought about the animals and other subjects they depicted.

Bushman beliefs

Informed researchers now accept that Bushman beliefs and rituals illuminate the art and afford a far more detailed understanding than any explanation that has gone before. The artists are now accorded their true dignity and worth, and, in sharp contrast to the older interpretations, the art is recognised as an astonishing intellectual and aesthetic achievement. How then do we know what the now-extinct Bushman painters and engravers believed? For decades it was thought that their beliefs had died with them towards the end of the last century. Fortunately, that is not entirely true.

Many of the Bushman beliefs we describe later were recorded in the 1870s by the Bleek family, who were at that time living in Cape Town. Dr Wilhelm Bleek (10), a German linguist, worked originally with

W.H.I. Bleek (Jagger Library).

/Xam Bushman convicts who had been sent from the Kenhardt district to work on a new breakwater in Table Bay. Later, some of these men brought their families to Cape Town, where they lived with the Bleeks at their Mowbray home. Bleek and his sister-in-law, Lucy Lloyd, took down nearly 12 000 pages of verbatim accounts of Bushman life, ritual and

A page from one of Lucy Lloyd's notebooks (Jagger Library).

myth. The actual Bushman words, recorded in a phonetic script Bleek himself developed, occupy one side of each page and a literal English translation the other (11). The /Xam language in these 12 000 pages is now extinct, but, thanks to the astonishing labours of the Bleek family, those Bushmen speak directly to us across more than a century.

In 1873, while the Bleek family was working in Cape Town, tumultuous events in Natal led altogether unexpectedly to further insights into Bushman belief and religion. The Hlubi chief Langalibalele refused to register guns his people had acquired. Knowing that this act of defiance would bring retribution, he withdrew into what is now Lesotho. The Natal Government called upon Joseph Millard Orpen, a magistrate in the northeastern Cape, to go into the mountains and try to head off Langalibalele. While his forces were being assembled, Orpen secured the services of a young Bushman guide named Qing, who 'had never seen a white man but in fighting'. Nevertheless, Orpen won his confidence and later wrote: 'When happy and at ease smoking over camp-fires, I got from him... stories and explanations of paintings, some of which he showed and I copied on our route.'

Although we do not have verbatim transcriptions such as those taken down by Wilhelm Bleek and Lucy Lloyd, these stories and explanations show that the Bushmen of the southeastern mountains had much in common with the /Xam Bushmen. Qing's authentic but somewhat enigmatic explanations of rock paintings are fundamental to any understanding of Bushman rock art.

To these invaluable collections we can add the research done on the Kalahari Bushmen during the last three decades. Writers such as the Marshalls, Richard Lee, Megan Biesele, Mathias Guenther, Philip Tobias, Alan Barnard, Marjorie Shostak, Richard Katz, Nancy Howell, Patricia Draper, George Silberbauer and Polly Wiessner have transformed the Bushmen from a relatively unknown people into one of the best-documented hunter-gatherer societies in the world.

Although the Kalahari Bushmen live far from much of the art and have no artistic tradition, comparison with the Bleek and Orpen collections shows that they preserve many of the extinct artists' beliefs and rituals. This important discovery came as a surprise, but it seems that the fundamental, underpinning beliefs of Bushman society were very widespread and of great antiquity. The paintings of, say, the Drakensberg and the western Cape, whatever their differences may be, sprang from the same fundamental system of beliefs. The quantity and essential unity of the Bushman records mean that we can no longer use ignorance as an excuse for self-indulgent guessing about southern African rock art.

As long ago as 1874, when he first saw Orpen's article on what he had learned from Qing, Wilhelm Bleek recognised the vital link between the art and Bushman beliefs:

The fact of Bushman paintings, illustrating Bushman mythology, has first been publicly demonstrated by this paper of Mr Orpen's; and to me, at all events, it was previously quite unknown, although I had hoped that such paintings might be found. This fact can hardly be valued sufficiently. It gives at once to Bushman art a higher character, and teaches us to look upon its products not as the mere daubing of figures for idle pastime, but as an attempt, however imperfect, at a truly artistic conception of the ideas which most deeply moved the Bushman mind, and filled it with religious feelings.

Bleek, who knew the Bushmen so well, had no misgivings about their intellectual capacity. Nor did he doubt that Bushman beliefs, such as those recorded by Orpen and himself, would unlock the mysteries of the art. Yet for decades writers have ignored or paid only the most superficial attention to these sources.

One reason for their omission to use genuine Bushman beliefs is that the sources are seldom easy to understand. One must remember that they are not in any way comparable with explanations expressed in Western terms and language by anthropologists. Rather, they are statements given by Bushmen themselves in their own manner of speaking and expressed in Bushman concepts and language. Their statements are therefore like the art itself: both are characteristically Bushman expressions of Bushman ideas, and both require careful study if we are to 'translate' them into language Westerners can understand. If we do not appreciate this problem, we end up playing a naive game of snap in which misunderstood Bushman ideas are matched with equally misunderstood paintings and engravings.

To understand what we are up against, we have only to ask ourselves what Bushmen would make of the English idiom 'raining cats and dogs'. They would have to accept, perhaps after initial hilarity, that we were speaking metaphorically and not literally. This sort of potential misunderstanding is exemplified by an explanation J.M. Orpen obtained. He asked his guide, Qing, about paintings of men with rhebuck heads. Qing replied:

They were men who had died and now lived in rivers, and were spoilt at the same time as the elands and by the dances of which you have seen paintings.

For many years this was taken to mean that the paintings depicted mythological spirits of the dead who, in tales now lost, lived in rivers. Today we know that the statement is, like the English 'raining cats and dogs', metaphorical, though the extent to which the Bushmen would have recognised it as metaphorical is not clear, any more than Westerners would see the statement 'the fashion has died out' as metaphorical. In fact, Qing's statement is a series of three metaphors (death, underwater, spoilt), each of which tells us something about the religious dance which linked men and eland. The precise meaning of these metaphors will become clearer when we later look beneath the surface of both the art and the relevant Bushman beliefs. Bushman thought and art are seldom, if ever, as simple as they first appear.

Because of the difficulties involved in finding the underlying connections between Bushman thought and art, many writers abandoned the Bushman records and relied on their own highly fallible intuition. They thought that one guess about the art was as good as another, that all 'theories' deserved equal acceptance, and that, ultimately, we would never know what the art meant because the artists had died a long time ago. For those archaeologists who precisely measure stone implements and work with radio-carbon dates, rock art research seemed a very vague and unscientific enterprise.

This is no longer true. We now recognise that, even though the artists are all dead, we do know a great deal about the Bushmen, and we judge explanations by how true they are to authentic Bushman beliefs and rituals.

This is not to say that we know everything we wish to know about Bushman rock art – far from it. But it does mean that we can safely reject and forget about those explanations that denigrate the Bushmen and take their art to mean what it appears to mean to Westerners. The range of possible explanations has been sharply reduced.

Recent research

Today, an explanation that derives from the most important Bushman ritual is widely accepted as the general framework in which the art should be understood. This explanation is that both paintings and engravings were closely associated with the activities of Bushman medicine people, or shamans. It is, in fact, Bushman beliefs about shamans that explain the animal characteristics, the hairs and the trailing streamers of the enigmatic Mlambonja painting with which this introduction started.

'Shaman' is a Tungus word from central Asia. It has been accepted in the anthropological literature to mean someone in a hunter-gatherer society who enters a trance in order to heal people, foretell the future,

Circular trance dance being performed in the Kalahari (photo: L. Marshall).

control the weather, ensure good hunting, and so forth. Some societies have only a few shamans, whereas others, like the Bushmen, have many. Some – not all – shamans in North America and Asia seem to suffer from psychological disabilities and play little part in general social life. By contrast, Bushman shamans are ordinary people who also perform all the everyday tasks that those who do not have their supernatural abilities perform. Bushman shamans are not a privileged class.

Because the shamanistic explanation of southern African rock art is deeply rooted in Bushman thought and because it fits the art so well, it is unlikely that it will be overthrown, although details and aspects of it will doubtless be refined as we continue to unravel the symbols, metaphors and implications of Bushman shamanism. It is probably true to say that no professional archaeologist or anthropologist familiar with Bushman rock art seriously questions the general validity of this explanation.

Bushman shamans sometimes exercise their supernatural powers in the solitary world of dreams, but in Bushman society shamanism is practised principally at a trance dance. At one of these dances, women, usually sitting around a central fire, clap the rhythm of special songs. The men dance in a circle around the women. Bushmen believe that the sounds of their dancing rattles and thudding steps combine with the women's insistent songs to activate a supernatural potency that resides in the songs and in the shamans themselves. When this potency 'boils' and rises up the shamans' spines, they enter trance. Today Bushmen hardly ever use hallucinogens, but they may have done so in the past. Instead, they rely on hyperventilation, intense concentration and highly rhythmic dancing to alter their state of consciousness. Experienced shamans can control their level of trance and move around curing people, but others sometimes crash to the ground unconscious. As in one of the metaphors Qing used, people in deep trance are said to be 'spoilt'.

During this state of trance, Bushman shamans perform their tasks, the most important of which is to cure people of known as well as unperceived ailments. They lay their trembling hands on all present to draw sickness out of people and into their own bodies. Then, with a high-pitched shriek, they expel the sickness through a 'hole' in the nape of the neck, the *n//au* spot. The sickness thus returns to its source, which is thought to be unidentified malevolent shamans and the ever-threatening but only vaguely identified spirits of the dead. Other important tasks, also said to be performed in trance, include rain-making, visiting distant camps on out-of-body travel, and control of animals. All these shamanistic activities are depicted in the art and are explained more fully in the next section of this book.

But to appreciate better the relationship between Bushman shamanism and art we must first examine more closely the supernatural potency that makes shamanistic work possible. The southern /Xam Bushman word for shaman, *!gi:xa*, emphasises the importance of potency. The first part of the word, *!gi:*, means potency, and the suffix, *-xa*, means 'full of', as in the English word 'powerful'. Today the !Kung of northern Botswana and Namibia use the phrase *n/um k"au*. *N/um* is their word for potency, and *k"au* means 'owner'.

A shaman was, thus, a person who was full of potency. But many other things, including the large game animals, were also thought to be imbued with potency. Lorna Marshall, who worked with the !Kung, likens potency to electricity: harnessed it can be useful, but uncontrolled or in too great an intensity it can be dangerous. The shamans' task is to control it for the good of all people.

Today about half the men and a third of the women in a Kalahari Bushman camp may be shamans. The Bleek records suggest that this was also the case among the nineteenth century southern /Xam. Most young men desire to become shamans, not for personal gain, but because they will be able to serve the

Trancedancers in the Kalahari (photo: L. Marshall).

community in that capacity. In their middle or late teens they go to an experienced shaman and ask him to teach them. The time of apprenticeship may last some years, during which the novice will dance with the older man, absorbing his potency.

After several years, the quest becomes more earnest, and there is much talk about the painful nature of the potency young men acquire. A !Kung man told Richard Katz: 'The young ones fear n/um and cry out. They cry tears. They cry out, "It's painful! It hurts!"' By the age of thirty-five they will know whether they will be able to conquer the pain and fear to become effective shamans. For some the pain and the experiences that await them in the spirit world are so terrifying that they abandon the quest.

Men who give up are not despised by the community; people recognise that trance is very painful and that controlling it is not for everyone. Nevertheless, those who fail feel their inadequacy. A man who had failed to become a shaman told Katz: 'It's awful to have to sit by and look at a sick child and say, "Why can't I help this child?"' Others persevere, going to as many dances as possible and dancing with great intensity. As they near the threshold of trance and the pain is almost unbearable, they run wildly into the bush and throw burning sticks at the spirits. Other people run after them and guide them back to the dance to prevent them from injuring themselves.

Sometimes, as they are circling the fire and the clapping women, they see spirit animals attracted by the dance standing out in the darkness. They direct one another's attention to these animals, pooling their experiences of the spirit world. They have come to terms with the experience, as nearly as anyone can.

And, from their own accounts, it is certainly an overwhelming experience. At first, one man told Katz: 'I see all the people like very small birds, the whole place will be spinning around and that is why we run around. The trees will be circling also.' Then, by passing underground, the shaman leaves the spinning world and enters the spirit world – the smell of burning flesh, men transformed into lions, grotesque spirits of the dead, biting snakes, bees and locusts, and then god himself, terrifying and foul. An old shaman told Megan Biesele that the only way a person could survive in this dreadful place was to become a mamba. In god's house, he added, there are lions, giraffes, leopards, zebras, elands, gemsboks and kudus. 'These things don't kill each other. They are god's possessions.' There, where god is smoking spirits of the recently dead over a special fire, the shaman pleads, at great risk to himself, for the lives of the sick.

Then, travelling again through the ground, the shaman returns to his earthly body. While he has been away, the people have cared for his body, rubbing it with sweat and dusting it with aromatic herbs. Exhausted, he falls into a deep, natural sleep.

The next day, fully recovered, he may tell the people about his experiences, and they will listen attentively, believing that they are hearing an authentic revelation of what the ultimate world – the spirit world – is like. Even though such accounts may be contradictory, each is accepted. After all, the spirit world is, in their view, beyond humankind's comprehension: all things are possible.

Everyone is permitted to hear these accounts of the spirit world; there is nothing esoteric about Bushman religion. Perhaps the art was, at least in part, another way in which shamans communicated their spiritual visions to their people. In the Kalahari today, Bushman religion is to a large degree idiosyncratic. In other words, shamans and other people have their own ideas about god and the spirit world. All these ideas, which often come to people in dreams and trance visions, are accepted, provided that they fall within the general framework of Bushman religion. So too for the art. Some painted or engraved revelations about the spirit world became accepted and widely depicted; others remained unique or rare, and thus idiosyncratic. For example, a crab was used (once only, as far as we know) to represent a shaman (67). When looking at Bushman rock art, we should always be alert to kinds of depiction that have never been found before and that represent the insights of particular shaman-artists.

Indeed, because so many of the paintings depict trance visions in considerable detail, it is likely that many, possibly all, artists were shamans. On the other hand, it seems improbable that shamans made the paintings and engravings while they were actually in trance. If the trance behaviour one can observe in the Kalahari is anything to go by, the shaman-artists of old would not have had sufficient self-control while in trance to produce such delicate art. It is more probable that they remembered and then depicted their experiences while in a normal state of consciousness, just as they describe their trance experiences in the Kalahari today. In addition to trance hallucinations, shamans in other parts of the world also experience after-images which may recur for many months after a trance experience. These after-images may last for a few seconds or up to a few minutes. They seem to float before one; or, if one is looking at a flat surface like a wall or a ceiling, they are like colour slides projected on a screen. Projected onto the wall of a rock shelter, such mental images could have provided the inspiration for painting. Like Wordsworth's concept of poetry, Bushman rock art was probably powerful emotion recollected in tranquillity.

If people other than shamans did paint, they seem to have drawn their topics from the same shamanistic repertoire. But any suggestion that people other than shamans painted was denied by an old Bushwoman, very possibly the last survivor of the southern Drakensberg Bushmen. She was well into her eighties when she was interviewed in 1985. Her life story was fascinating. In the last century some Bushman families, of which hers was one, went to live with Xhosa and Pondomise chiefs to act as rain-makers. This woman's father had been a shaman, and her sister, who had died some eight years before she was interviewed, had been the last of the line of rain-makers. Although her recollections of her youth were imperfect, she was able to identify paintings done by her father, to describe various rituals, and to confirm that eland blood had been used in the manufacture of paint. She went on to insist that *all* the paintings had been done by shamans. Other people, she said, did not paint.

She explained that, as people danced, they turned to face the paintings when they wished to heighten the level of their potency. Then, in the cave where she had lived as a child, she danced once more and turned to the paintings her father had made so many years before. Singing in a low, monotonous tone, she was transported back to the days of eland power.

Through the use of blood from highly potent animals, such as eland, the shaman-painters infused their paint with potency. For the Bushmen, potency flowed from the animal, via its blood, to the paintings where it was stored, and then from the paintings to trancing shamans. Painted sites were thus storehouses of the potency that made contact with the spiritual world possible, that guaranteed humankind's existence by facilitating healing, rain-making and animal control, and that, by flowing between nature and people, gathered up all aspects of life in a single spiritual unity. One should not, however, think of the sites as sacred shrines to be approached by a select few only. Most were also places where people lived and conducted their daily affairs. Bushmen do not draw a clear distinction between the sacred and the secular: for them the spiritual realm is as real and immediate as the physical. The art, which reflects the spiritual realm, brought that world into the midst of this world.

When viewing Bushman rock art, we should remind ourselves that we are looking at a bridge between two worlds. The structure of that bridge is intricate; the following pages give only an outline. As research progresses, we expect to learn more and more about the spiritual panorama preserved on the rocks of southern Africa. The creature that gazes out over Natal from the Mlambonja boulder (1) is not as enigmatic as it was even a decade ago. It came from the very heart of Bushman religious experience.

PART II

Detailed explanations

The illustrations of Bushman paintings in this section are accurate tracings. This technique of recording rock paintings is, in many instances, preferable to photography because it clearly shows faint and minute details that the camera cannot easily capture. These very details are often important clues to the meaning of the depictions.

The illustrations are monochrome reductions of the colourful originals. Stippling is used to show variations in colour, fading, and the shading of one colour into another; readers should bear in mind that stippling is not a feature of the original paintings. A dashed line represents flake scars, while a line of alternating dashes and dots indicates other features on the rock face such as steps, hollows and cracks.

The illustrations of rock engravings are rubbings made in a manner similar to brass rubbings. They show the engraving itself and the texture of the rock.

These paintings and engravings have been chosen because they clearly illustrate important features of the art. For the most part, they represent categories of depiction, further examples of which can be found at many sites. The accompanying explanations are thus not restricted to these specific depictions.

THE TRANCE DANCE

14. This is one of the clearest Bushman paintings of a shamanistic curing ritual. In the centre a person lies supine with knees drawn up, while a kneeling shaman lays his hands on him. Around these two people there is a crescentric line that may represent a hut or part of the furrow produced by the dancing men. On the other hand, it may not be a 'realistic' feature (18; 28; 41a; 41b; 67a; 67b).

Similarly, the scatter of arrows may not be 'real' arrows because Bushmen never leave such dangerous things lying around (52). More probably, they are 'arrows of sickness'. These are said to be small, invisible arrows that malevolent shamans shoot into people whom they wish to make ill. They may even be in a person without his or her knowing it. At a curing ritual, a shaman draws them out of people into his own body and then expels them.

Not all dances are circular like this one. Sometimes the shamans dance in the centre, while the women, standing or sitting around them, clap the rhythm of the dance. Many paintings show neither of these forms (15; 28); instead, the dancers are in a long line. Perhaps the artists, who did not use perspective as we know it, simply strung out the

38

circular movement. On the other hand, these paintings may not be in any sense a 'photograph' of a real dance but rather a depiction of the essence of the activity.

14

15. This dance is of the linear kind. It also has numerous significant details. Most important are the lines coming from the dancers' noses. When a Bushman shaman enters trance, he or she sometimes suffers a nosebleed. The /Xam people told Wilhelm Bleek that the shamans rubbed this blood on their patients in the belief that its smell would protect them from sickness. Nasal blood is one of the chief features by which to identify trancing shamans, and every figure should be carefully examined for it.

Another important feature is the bending-forward posture. As a shaman's potency begins to 'boil', his stomach muscles contract into a tight, painful knot and he bends forward, sometimes with his torso at right angles to his legs. In this position he often supports his weight on one or two dancing sticks. Here some of the dancers are carrying decorated sticks.

At the extreme right, a dancer's fingers are painted partially on the ceiling of the shelter, and long lines extend from them over the viewer's head. These lines probably represent the sickness, invisible to ordinary people, that shamans remove and cast into the darkness from where it came.

Perhaps the most interesting feature here is the eland head. It represents the potency that shamans harness to enter trance. It may be a 'real' head, but its isolation suggests that it is rather a symbol of potency. The head, the lines on the ceiling, and the arrows of sickness in 14 suggest that paintings like these depict a shaman's privileged view of the real and the non-real elements of a trance dance.

15

16a. Neither 14 nor 15 has depictions of women, but they are often painted. Usually they are seated and clapping, with their fingers individually drawn. Unlike Westerners, Bushwomen do not clap with the hands across one another and the fingers together. Instead they hold their hands parallel, with the fingers splayed out and bent slightly backwards. This is exactly how they are frequently painted. By clapping in this way they produce a sharp, explosive sound. Every depiction of a clapping woman signifies the activation of potency.

16b. A distinctive dancing posture has the hands held up at about head height. Dancing in this manner and concentrating intensely, shamans move towards the threshold of trance. Men are dancing in this position in 14 and 15.

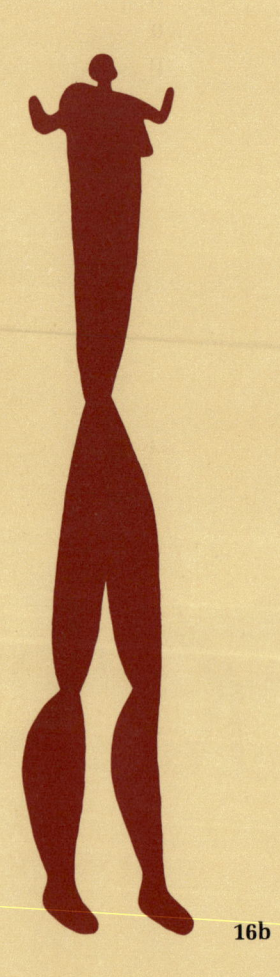

16b

16c. Sometimes postures are combined. Here an elegantly painted and somewhat elongated (34) figure holds its hands above its head (16b) and also bends forward (15) as its potency 'boils'.

16d. This dancer is holding a flywhisk, an important accessory for the dance. It is used to provide an aesthetically pleasing sense of balance, but also to keep arrows of sickness at bay. Lorna Marshall noticed that flywhisks are used only at trance dances. They are therefore another significant indicator of trance.

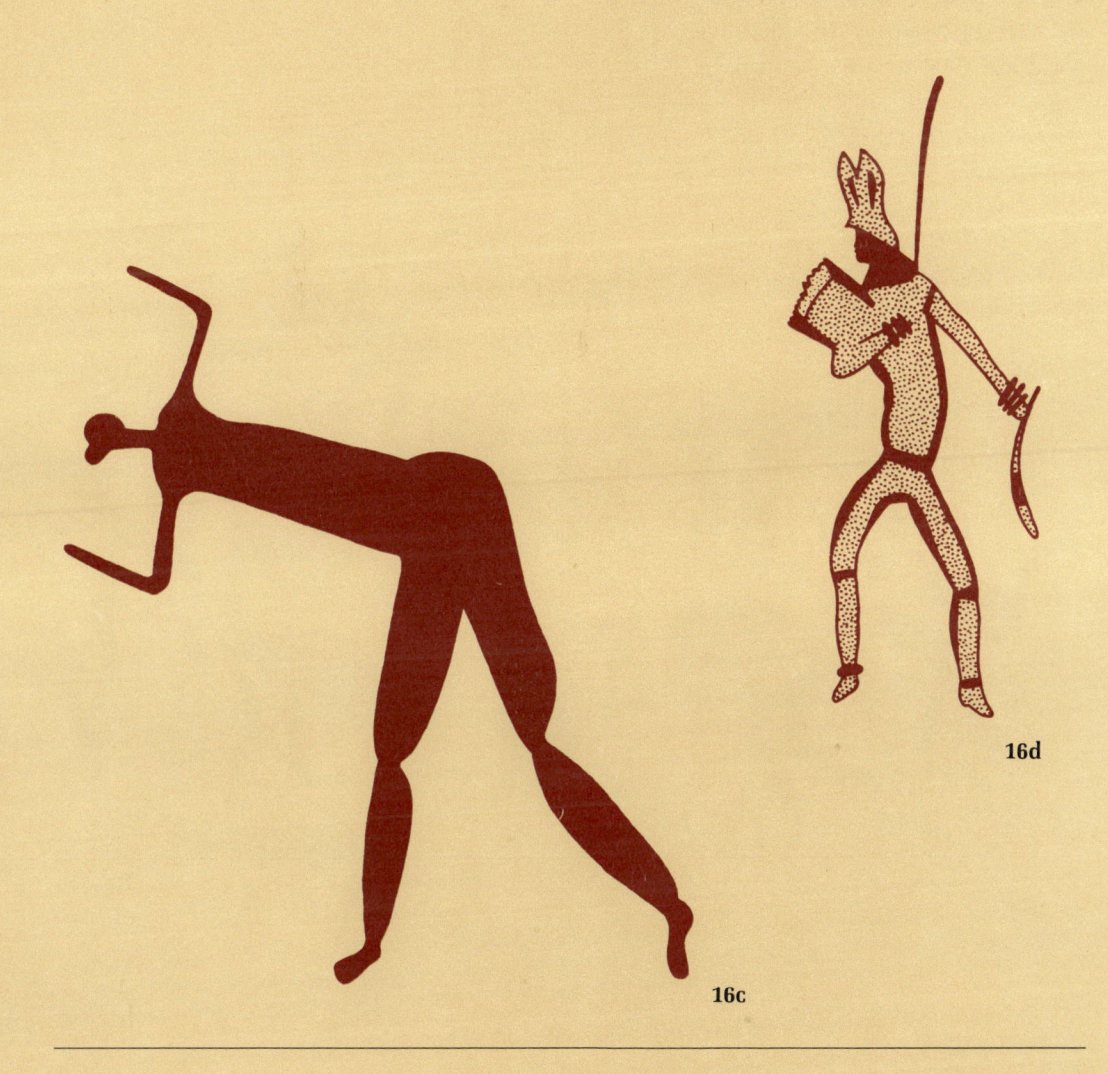

In **17**, a lively group dances in the bending-forward posture. Some have trance blood falling from the nose (15), and one supports his weight on two sticks. Most have dancing rattles wound around their calves. Today, these are made from strings of dried cocoons or seed pods filled with pebbles or pieces of ostrich eggshell. The /Xam people also made rattles from dried springbok ears. In this painting, the ears or cocoons are individually and minutely drawn. As the men dance, they produce an evocative swishing sound. The rattles are considered to have potency and are sometimes shaken along a person's back to extract 'arrows of sickness' (14).

Some dancers have their arms parallel to their bodies, while one on the extreme left has its arms extended backwards. Some shamans, a !Kung man explained, hold their arms backwards when they are asking god to put more potency into their bodies. Like nasal blood, this posture is one of the clearest indications of trance and is often painted.

One man in a sitting position wears a kaross (skin cloak). A /Xam man told Lucy Lloyd:

> *A man who is a sorcerer will not lay down his kaross, even if it is hot, because he knows that the place will not seem hot to him, for his inside is cold... For the doings of sorcerers are not easy.*

All around the dancers there are white flecks that probably depict potency. At a dance, trancing shamans, but no one else, can see both potency and sickness. This scene thus also has an element that suggests it depicts a shaman's, rather than an ordinary person's, view of a dance.

We have already noted the role of women in singing and clapping the rhythm of medicine songs and thus activating potency (16a). But some were also respected curers in their own right. One of Wilhelm Bleek and Lucy Lloyd's informants spoke of a female shaman called !Kwara-an who, like other /Xam shamans, sniffed or 'snored' sickness out of people:

> !Kwara-an, when she snored me, took something out of my liver. Stooping she took the thing outside; then she went to lie down outside with it. She came back again stooping, for she meant to heal for me the place from which she had taken the thing... while blood came from her nose. She took the blood which she had sneezed out with the thing and rubbed me with it, for she wanted me to have that blood's scent.

!Kwara-an also explained that she had to look after herself in case she lost her ability to cure:

> She did not eat bad things, but was careful as to her food, lest she eat ashes with it, for if she ate things which were not clean, she would become weak; her snoring power would leave her.

The /Xam word translated as 'snoring power' also means 'nose' (11): power was located in the place from which trance blood flowed and which sniffed out sickness.

Another /Xam female shaman, Tãnõ-!khauken, had different supernatural powers:

> My aunt used to turn herself into a lion and seek us, as she wanted to see whether we were still where we lived. When she smelt the scent of our hut, she passed before it and roared like a lioness, because she wanted us to hear her, that it was she who had come to look for us.

18. This dance group seems to emphasise female shamans, some of whom lie on the ground bleeding from the nose. One apparently male figure is associated with the white line that encircles the women. This line is another of the non-real features that challenge a purely literal interpretation of even seemingly 'realistic', almost photographic, paintings. It seems that even the most 'ordinary' paintings are actually showing the shamans' privileged view of things. Their visions are combined with their ordinary perceptions of their surroundings. When looking at rock paintings, we should always be alert to these easily missed elements.

The shamanistic role of women seems to be increasing in the Kalahari today. At the beginning of this century, the women's Drum Dance started, and it is now spreading more rapidly than ever and gaining in popularity. In it the usual roles are reversed: the women dance in more or less one place while the men play the rhythm on a long drum. Although the women enter trance, they do not cure during the Drum Dance. Some say that the Drum Dance is a 'school' where they learn to trance, and some of them indeed go on to become shamans.

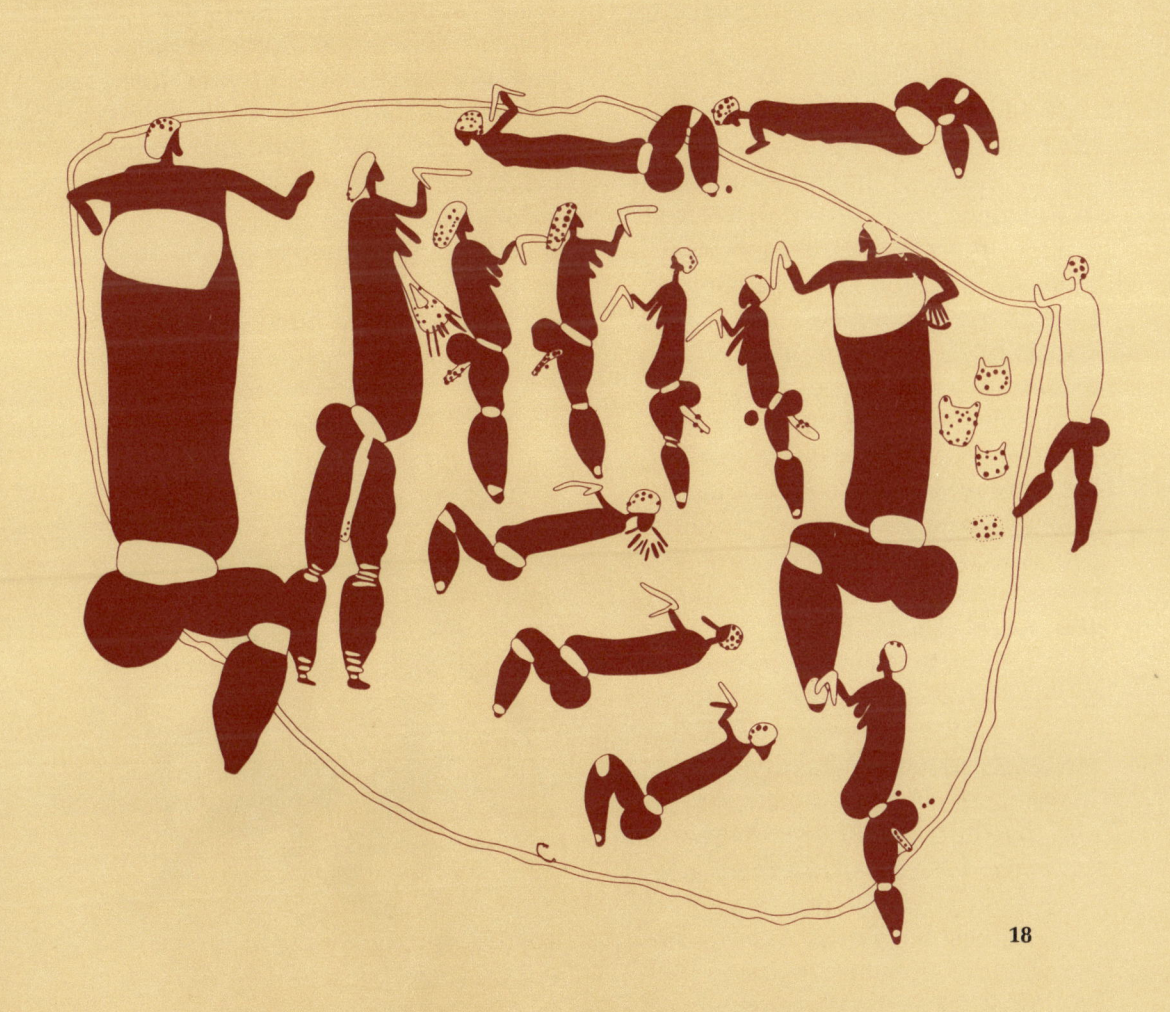

18

Once the numerous postures and gestures of trance are identified, they turn up frequently and over wide geographical areas. In some ways they may be likened to the stylised postures of Western heraldry or religious art. Each has its own significance. For instance, in Western religious art a hand raised with two fingers extended signifies preaching or blessing.

19a. In Bushman rock art, one such repeated posture is a hand raised to the nose or face. As we have seen (11, 15), the nose had important meaning in Bushman shamanism: it was used for 'sniffing' out sickness, and the word itself was sometimes used metaphorically to mean the power to cure (11). Here, a standing, possibly dancing, man is next to a seated man with a bow. In the Kalahari, a man who has had no success in hunting for some while may ask a shaman to cure him and restore his luck. This painting seems to depict such a circumstance.

19b. Another significant gesture is a pointing finger. Lorna Marshall was told that a shaman 'must not point his finger fixedly at anyone or snap his finger at anyone, especially a child... "A fight" might go along his arm, leap into the child, and kill it.' 'A fight' is a metaphor for a particularly strong concentration of potency. Katz noted that, in teaching a novice to trance, an experienced shaman may snap his fingers at the student's stomach; each snap signifies an arrow. During a particularly intense episode of a dance, a shaman stopped, turned and pointed his finger at another dancer across the fire. The dancer immediately fell over. Later the shaman repeated the action with the same effect.

An old southern Drakensberg Bushwoman (p. 36) said that shamans simply pointed at dassies (rock rabbits), the dassies 'froze', and the men then walked over to them and picked them up. It is possible that some of the painted pointing fingers convey this belief about the shamans' control over animals (46, 47). The woman spoke only of dassies, but Bleek was told that people pointed a burning stick of a medicine plant at springbok so that they would run

19a

slowly and easily fall to the hunters' arrows.

19c. Another oft-repeated posture is a raised knee, here combined with a pointing finger. It may be related to the tightening of the stomach muscles in trance (15).

It is very important to remember that Bushman artists often used these and other features in contexts that are not clearly dance scenes. This is because numerous activities are said to be performed by people who have entered the spirit world of trance. Sometimes, for instance, there may be a line of walking figures, only one of whom bleeds from the nose or has a hand raised to the nose. But this one figure is sufficient to tell us that we are looking at a trancing group. The apparent diversity of the art that led some researchers to conclude that it is simply a record of diverse daily affairs is in fact contained within the wide range of shamanistic activities and experiences.

19c

19b

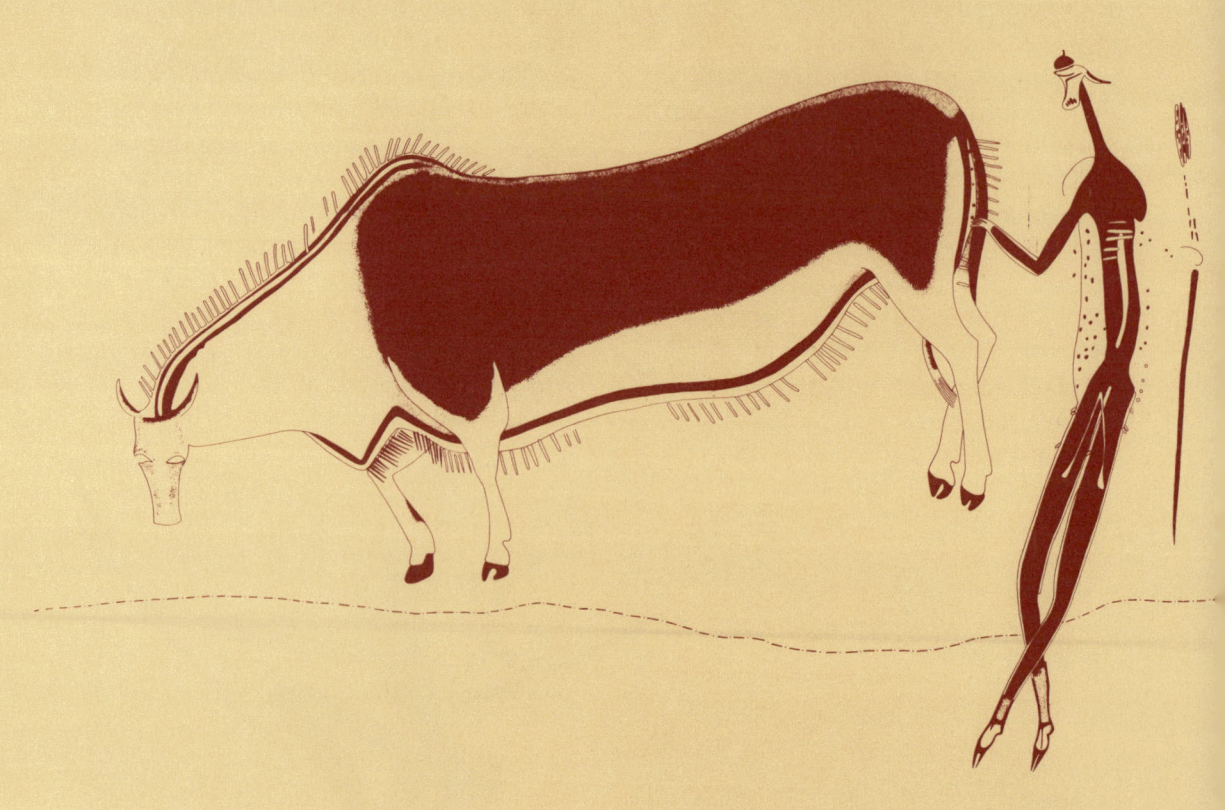

METAPHORS OF TRANCE

Death

The experience of trance is so overwhelming and so difficult to describe that people have to use metaphors – that is, they have to compare their experience with some more familiar experience that others can understand. In Western society, people use such expressions as 'a trip' to describe altered states of consciousness. The commonest Bushman metaphor for trance is 'death'. They say that shamans 'die' when they cross over into the spirit world, and trance itself is sometimes called 'half death'.

One of the ways in which the artists depicted this metaphor was through animal behaviour. They noticed a striking similarity between a 'dying' shaman and an antelope, especially an eland, dying from the effects of a poisoned arrow. Both the shaman and the eland tremble violently, stagger, lower their heads, bleed from the nose, sweat excessively and, finally, collapse

50

20. A dying eland lowers its head and has exaggerated hair standing up over much of its body. When an animal reaches this stage, its neck muscles relax and its head swings from side to side; here it faces the viewer. The forelegs are giving way under the animal's weight, and the hindlegs are crossed as it stumbles.

With this dying eland there are four shamans, three of whom have been transformed so that they share features of the eland (30). Two have hair standing on end, hoofs, and features of antelope heads. The one holding the eland's tail has his legs crossed in imitation of the eland's crossed legs. Above right, another shaman has an antelope head and fetlocks, and appears to be wearing a kaross. The animal characteristics of these figures show that their 'death' is analogous to the death of the eland with which they are painted and that, in this 'death', they become like the eland. In Qing's phrase, they have been 'spoilt at the same time as the elands and by the dances'.

In the centre of the group, a dancer is in the bending-forward posture (15) and has its arms extended (17). Its head is raised and a short kaross hangs down from its neck. In contrast to the other figures, it is fairly 'realistic'. Its presence again stresses one of the principles of Bushman rock art: what we see on the rock is a blend of real and visionary elements. In other words, the art depicts the shamans' multidimensional view of reality.

20

unconscious. Moreover, an eland's hair stands on end, and /Xam Bushmen spoke of hair growing on the back of a man in trance.

Many of these features of dying behaviour are depicted in the art, where they are used to link 'dying' shamans to potent but dying animals. Orpen's guide, Qing, referred to this 'death' when he said that the men with rhebuck heads (30), had been 'spoilt [i.e., entered into deep trance, p. 29] at the same time as the elands and by the dances of which you have seen paintings'.

51

Most of the features of antelope dying-behaviour we have so far examined – staggering, sweat, trembling, nasal blood, lowered head – are also displayed by a shaman entering trance. There are some other characteristics of dying antelope that are not shared by 'dying' shamans. These are painted less frequently, but they are no less important.

21a. When shown a copy of this painting, a !Kung man explained that, as arrow poison starts to take effect, an antelope's leg muscles often go into spasm so that it staggers along with a rear leg extended or dragging. This antelope's head is also lowered in the more familiar dying posture.

21b. To show that even this less commonly depicted dying behaviour was also used metaphorically by Bushman artists, we examine a visionary figure. It has an antelope head (30, 31) comparable with those in 20, and two appendages hang from its chest. It also has fetlocks instead of feet. One leg is extended stiffly to show that it is 'dying' in trance.

21c. In another behavioural characteristic, a dying eland lowers its head, but at the same time raises its nose. It does this because, as it is pursued, its nostrils become clogged with blood and foam and it cannot breathe normally. This eland is being pursued by a hunter, but the short bar across the man's penis suggests he is not merely a 'real' hunter. Some researchers have taken this feature ('infibulation', as it is sometimes called) to represent some sort of attachment to the penis, but the circumstances in which it is painted and some of its elaborations suggest that it is not 'realistic'.

Repeated postures such as these acquire general symbolic significance. Dying animals imply more than just physical death: they also recall the 'death' of shamans.

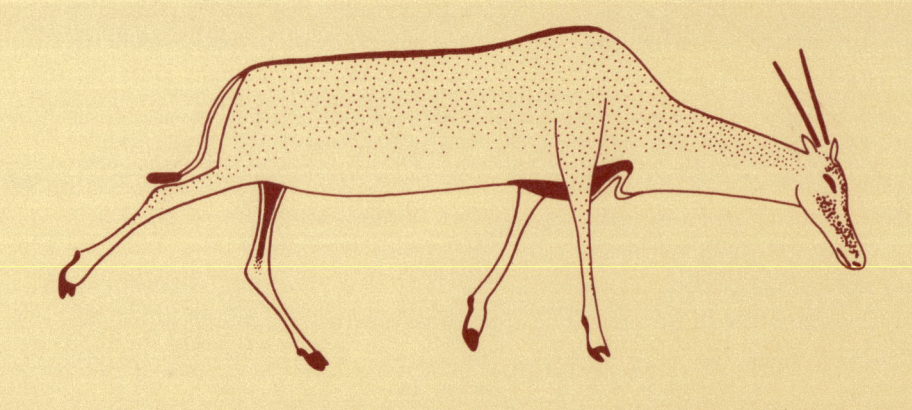

21a

52

Indeed, often one cannot be sure if one is looking at a 'real' dying eland or at a metaphorical depiction of a 'dying' shaman. 20 shows just how closely related the two are. The unity of the Bushman artistic system and the uniformity of its governing principles suggest that, whenever an oft-repeated and demonstrably metaphorical posture is depicted, it means more than just its literal implications. We should consider all its resonances.

It is not easy to be sure to what extent Bushmen themselves recognise 'death' as a metaphor and to what extent they use the phrase literally. For us it is entirely metaphorical (shamans do not *really* die), but for them it has at least an element of reality (shamans really do go to the spirit world).

21b

21c

Underwater

Another metaphor for trance experience is 'underwater'. Like 'death', being underwater has a number of parallels with trance. Both involve difficulty in breathing, sounds in the ears, affected vision, a sense of weightlessness, unusual perspectives and, finally, unconsciousness. Numerous accounts of trance experience show that the Bushmen link trance with being underwater.

For instance, an old trancer told Megan Biesele that, when the giraffe and god 'took' him into trance, they went to a 'wide body of water':

It was a river. He took me to the river. The two halves of the river lay to either side of us, one to the left and one to the right. God made the waters climb, and I lay my body in the direction they were flowing... My feet were behind, and my head was in front. That's how I lay. Then I entered the stream and began to move forward.

Wilhelm Bleek's /Xam Bushmen spoke of shamans entering waterholes rather than rivers and gave us further insights into what Bushman trance experience was like. During a trance rain-making ritual (42-45), a shaman's heart 'goes away dying':

Then his heart falls down into the waterpit... It enters water which also lives, as does he who is a sorcerer... For this is the water from which sorcerers are wont to fetch rainbulls... He really goes to the waterpit which is a big water.

This man explained that it was not ordinary water into which shamans went: it was 'alive'. And, like Megan Biesele's informant, he emphasised the size of the water.

A similar idea occurs in certain myths. The Mantis, the southern Bushman trickster-deity (p. 13), who is also a shaman, dives into a waterhole when he enters trance. When he comes out of the water, he sits on the bank and says, 'I am still wet, I must first dry.'

When Bushman artists wished to depict the aquatic metaphor, they turned to the animal world, as they did when they wished to depict 'death'. **22** shows a shaman with erect hair (20) and holding a flywhisk (16d). He is surrounded by fish and eels. The man's cloven hoofs (30, 31) and the curious line fringed with dots (41) show that the painting should not be interpreted literally: it does not depict a corpse being consumed by fish at the bottom of a river. Rather, it is a shaman who is 'underwater'. The fish and eels are thus part of the same system of ideas as the man's hoofs, flywhisk and erect hair. The apparently disparate elements of the painting actually fit together.

Depictions of fish and eels (32, 39a, 40) are not nearly as common as those of antelope, but they do occur throughout southern Africa, in both the paintings and the engravings.

22

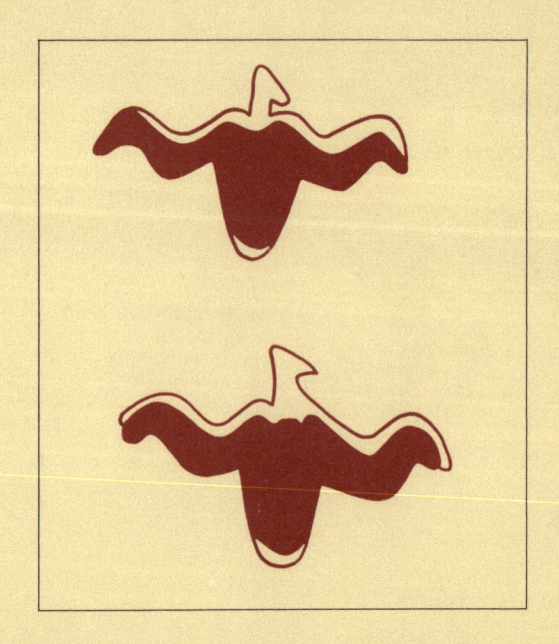

Flight

23. Trance is a very complex experience. Aspects of it can be interpreted in different ways by different people. Often these ways are governed by the culture and environment in which they live. Nevertheless, certain aspects of the experience are almost universally expressed by the same metaphor. One of these universal metaphors is 'flight'. For instance, it is now recognised by many historians that tales of mediaeval witches flying through the air derived from the experiences of altered consciousness.

The Bushmen, too, used the flight metaphor. As with other metaphors we have discussed, Bushman artists used members of the animal world when they wished to depict this metaphor. The painting here shows a rain-animal, part of Bushman rain-making rituals (42-45). To the right, there is a school of fish signifying 'underwater', and to the left is a group of birds signifying 'flight'. Two metaphors are thus brought together.

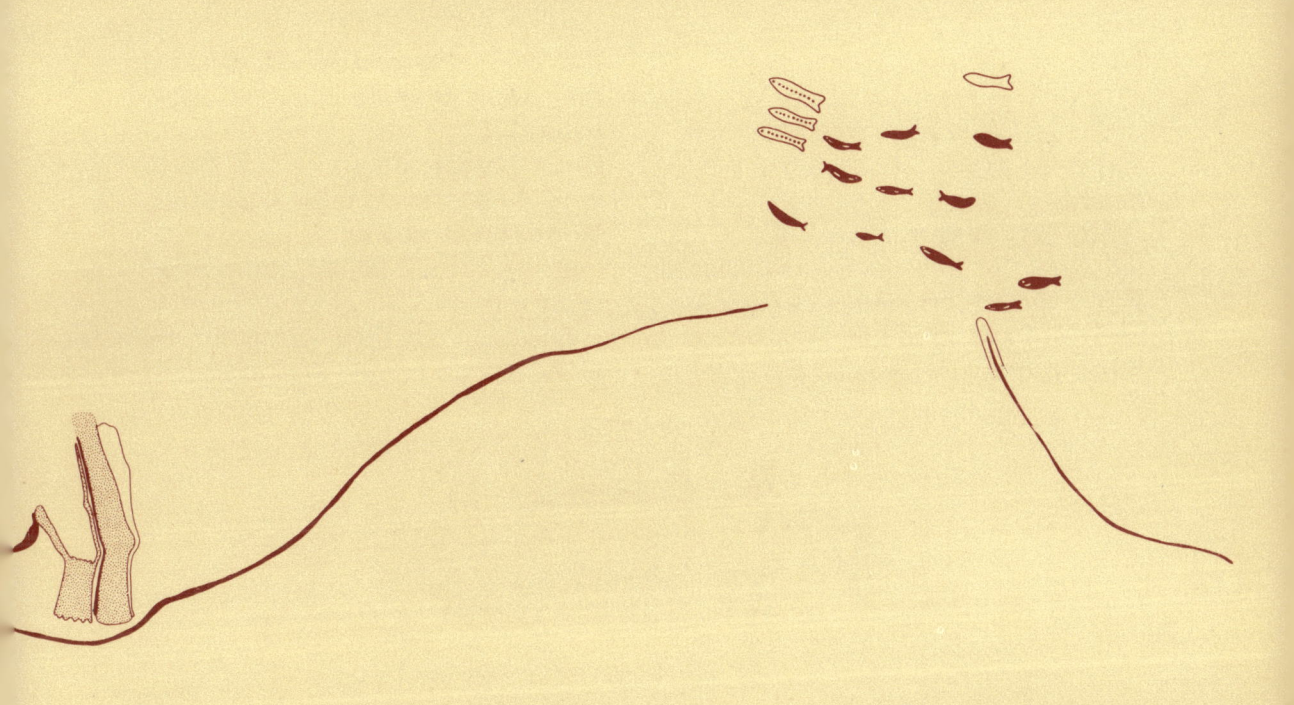

This dual concept also appears in the Mantis myths (p. 13). When the Mantis enters trance and before he dives into the waterhole, he sprouts feathers and flies.

Fight

The last metaphor we examine is 'fight'. To appreciate its force, we must first look at its background.

The very idea of a fight is terrifying for Bushmen. In so closely knit a society, friction is dangerous and can flare up at any moment. When it does, the women run to hide the men's poisoned arrows because they know that the slightest wound is fatal (52). Family quarrels can easily become public affairs. Social tension is economically disruptive because men should co-operate in hunting; if they do not, the whole camp suffers a shortage of meat.

Bushmen use their words for 'fight' to signify an intense concentration of

24

supernatural potency (p. 32, 34). Potency, although not in itself harmful, can, so they say, even kill a man if it is very intense. The !Kung also call such a concentration a 'death thing'.

An interesting use of this metaphor occurs in one of the Mantis myths. After the Meerkats had killed the Mantis's eland, they appropriated its potency (55-59). The Mantis then tried to fight against the 'eland's fight', as the narrator put it, but his arrows were deflected and flew back at him dangerously. The Meerkats were safely protected by the eland's 'fight', and even the creator of the eland was impotent. This incident is not just a whimsical tale: it is clearly a supernatural or trance fight between shamans (51, 63). The shaman Mantis shoots arrows of sickness (14) at the Meerkat shamans, but they are able to protect themselves with eland power.

24. In the /Xam language, the fighting eland in this painting would be *sā-ka /ā*, 'eland fight', a phrase that could metaphorically mean 'great eland potency'. The heads of the eland are lowered as they butt each other. The one on the right bleeds from a wound in the neck, and the other bleeds from the mouth or nose. The animals' strength in combat has been marvellously caught, and the placement of their legs on a sloping ledge of rock seems to give them added power.

That the artist actually intended the metaphorical meaning is confirmed by the juxtaposition of shamans. To the left, a shaman with eland tail, hoofs and head leans forward apparently to touch the back of one of the eland. He, like the eland, bleeds from the nose (15). He is participating so fully in the eland's potency that he is blending with the animal (30-31). The central figure to the right also bleeds from the nose and has hoofs. The eland on the left has an extra leg (35).

STAGES OF TRANCE

Some of the experiences we have so far discussed are so strange and bizarre that they are difficult for Westerners to comprehend. There is, however, a way of approaching them that sorts them into a series of three stages that are experienced by people as they go deeper and deeper into trance. These stages were discovered in the course of neuropsychological research conducted by Ronald Siegel and others into altered states of consciousness. The research was not in any way concerned with rock art, but, because all shamanism is based on altered states of consciousness, it is of the utmost importance to our attempt to understand Bushman rock art.

In the first place, we must remember that various factors can alter a person's state of consciousness. The neuro-psychological experiments were conducted largely with hallucinogens such as LSD. Nevertheless, the state of consciousness induced by this drug does not differ materially from the effects of a wide range of drugs or from the states induced by sensory deprivation, pain, rhythmic movement or sound, intense concentration, hyperventilation, and even, in some respects, migraine headaches. This means that, although Bushman shamans may not have depended on hallucinogens as heavily as shamans in other parts of the world do, their experiences would have been very similar to those of other shamans and also to those of Western subjects who take part in neuropsychological experiments.

The relevance of this research to shamanism in general is well demonstrated by the Tukano people of the Amazon Basin who regularly take the drug *yajé* (*Banisteriopsis*). When Geraldo Reichel-Dolmatoff asked them to describe their experiences, they spoke of stages that correlate well with those discovered in laboratory research. Even more surprising, when they were asked to draw their visions, they drew forms that were almost identical to those drawn by Western subjects in the experiments. Some trance experiences are human universals and, as we shall see, were depicted by Bushman shamans on the rocks of southern Africa.

Stage I: entoptics

25, 26. In the first stage of altered consciousness, people 'see' *entoptic phenomena*, or *entoptics*. These are luminous geometric shapes that include zigzags, chevrons, dots, grids, vortexes and nested U-shapes. All these percepts are experienced as incandescent, shimmering, moving, and sometimes as enlarging patterns. They also grade into one another and combine in a bewildering way. Because they derive from the actual structure of the human nervous system, all people who enter certain states of altered consciousness, no matter what their cultural background, are liable to perceive them.

Entoptic phenomena cannot be consciously controlled; they seem to have a life of their own. They are, furthermore, characterised by varied and saturated colours. Sometimes a bright light in the centre of vision obscures the forms, but peripheral images can still be observed. Another bewildering factor is the rapidity with which entoptics change. Laboratory subjects new to the experience find it difficult to keep pace with the rapid flow of imagery, but, significantly, training and familiarity with the experience increase their powers of observation.

The relevance of this neuropsychological research to Bushman rock art is clear. We already know that the artists were, at least in many instances, shamans who entered an altered state of consciousness and would therefore, like all other people in similar circumstances, have experienced entoptic phenomena. When we turn to the art, we find these very forms – grids, dots, zigzags and so on. For reasons not yet fully understood, it seems that there are more entoptics in their pure forms among the engravings than the paintings, but they certainly occur in both art forms.

Bushman shamans evidently 'saw' these forms in trance and then depicted them. This means that they

25

26

probably attached meanings to them. The Amazonian Tukano, for example, say that wavy parallel lines are 'the thought of the Sun-Father' and that parallel chains of small dots are the Milky Way, the first goal of ecstatic flight. We do not yet know what meanings Bushman shamans gave to their entoptics. The forms they saw were very similar to the ones seen by the Tukano, but, because their cultural background is different, the meanings they attached to them would also have been different.

An example is the flecks that sometimes surround trance scenes (17). Bushman shamans believe the place where a trance dance is performed to be redolent with potency that can be seen only by people in trance. The flickering dot and fleck entoptic, projected onto a shaman's normal vision of a dance,

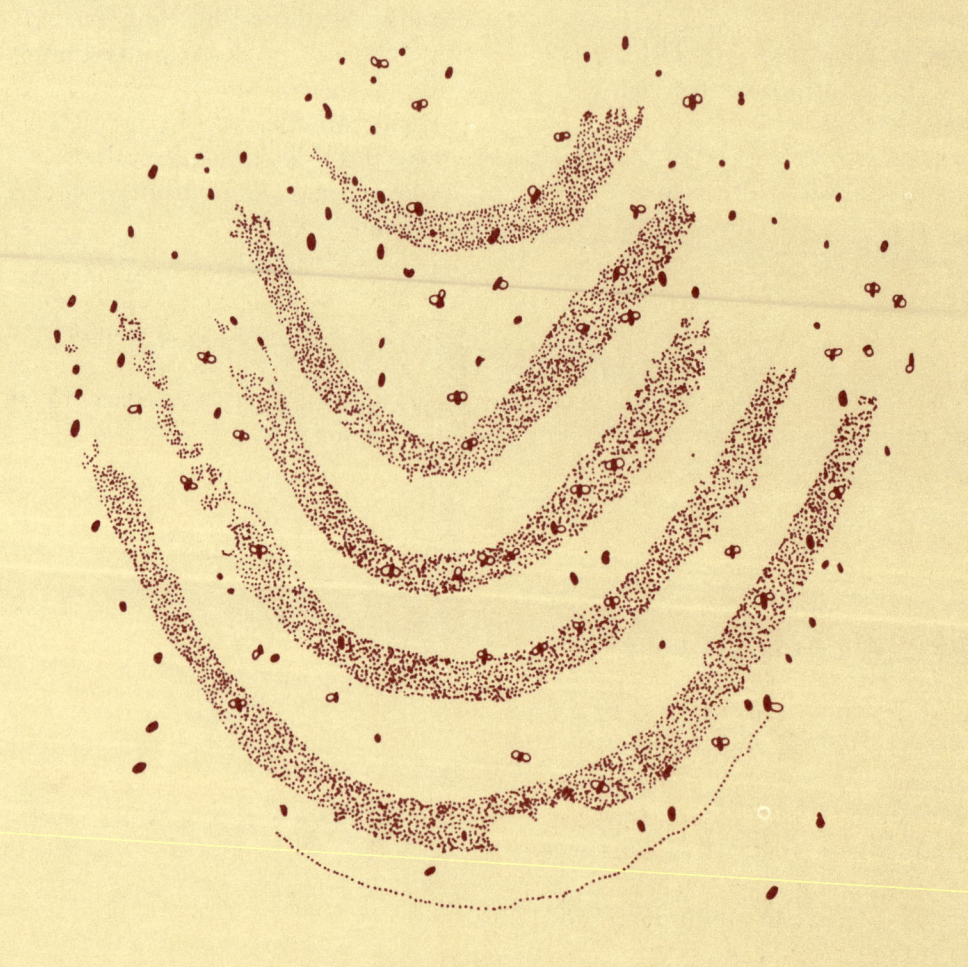

27a

may have sometimes been understood as that potency.

Stage II: construals

In the second stage of trance, people try to make sense of entoptic phenomena by elaborating them into objects with which they are familiar. In a normal state of consciousness the brain, receives a constant stream of messages from the five senses – sight, sound, smell, touch and hearing. A visual image (and, of course, other sensory information) reaching the brain is decoded by being matched against a store of experience. If a 'fit' can be effected, the image is 'recognised'. In altered states the nervous system itself becomes a 'sixth sense' that produces a variety of images, including entoptic phenomena. The brain attempts to recognise or decode these shapes even as it does impressions supplied by the nervous system in a normal state of consciousness. This process of making sense is linked to a person's state of mind and expectations. For instance, if a person is thirsty, an ambiguous round shape can be elaborated into a cup of water, or, if he or she is fearful, into an anarchist's bomb. Such elaborations are called *construals*.

27a. Bushman shamans reaching this stage of trance sometimes construed entoptics as things associated, in their society, with shamanism. For instance, honeycombs in the wild often assume the form of nested U-shapes that are like one of the entoptic forms (26). The accompanying bees in numerous painted examples of such curves suggest that some Bushman shamans interpreted the entoptic shapes as a honeycomb because bees are a Bushman symbol of potency (p. 34). This construal of U-shapes was thus controlled by beliefs about trance performance. It was probably also encouraged by a buzzing in the ears experienced in certain altered states (22). All five senses, not just vision, hallucinate in trance, and the aural hallucination of buzzing is variously construed by people around the world as bees, rushing wind, falling water and so forth.

27b. In this painting another entoptic, a zigzag, has been transformed into a buck-headed serpent (62). The blood falling from the noses of some such serpents links them to shamans (15).

27b

28. In this dance scene a man at the right and a woman above right bleed from the nose (15). Above the dancers are a swarm of bees and a rectangular shape that may be a hive. In the Kalahari today, Bushmen still like to dance when the bees are swarming because they believe that they can harness their potency for a particularly effective dance.

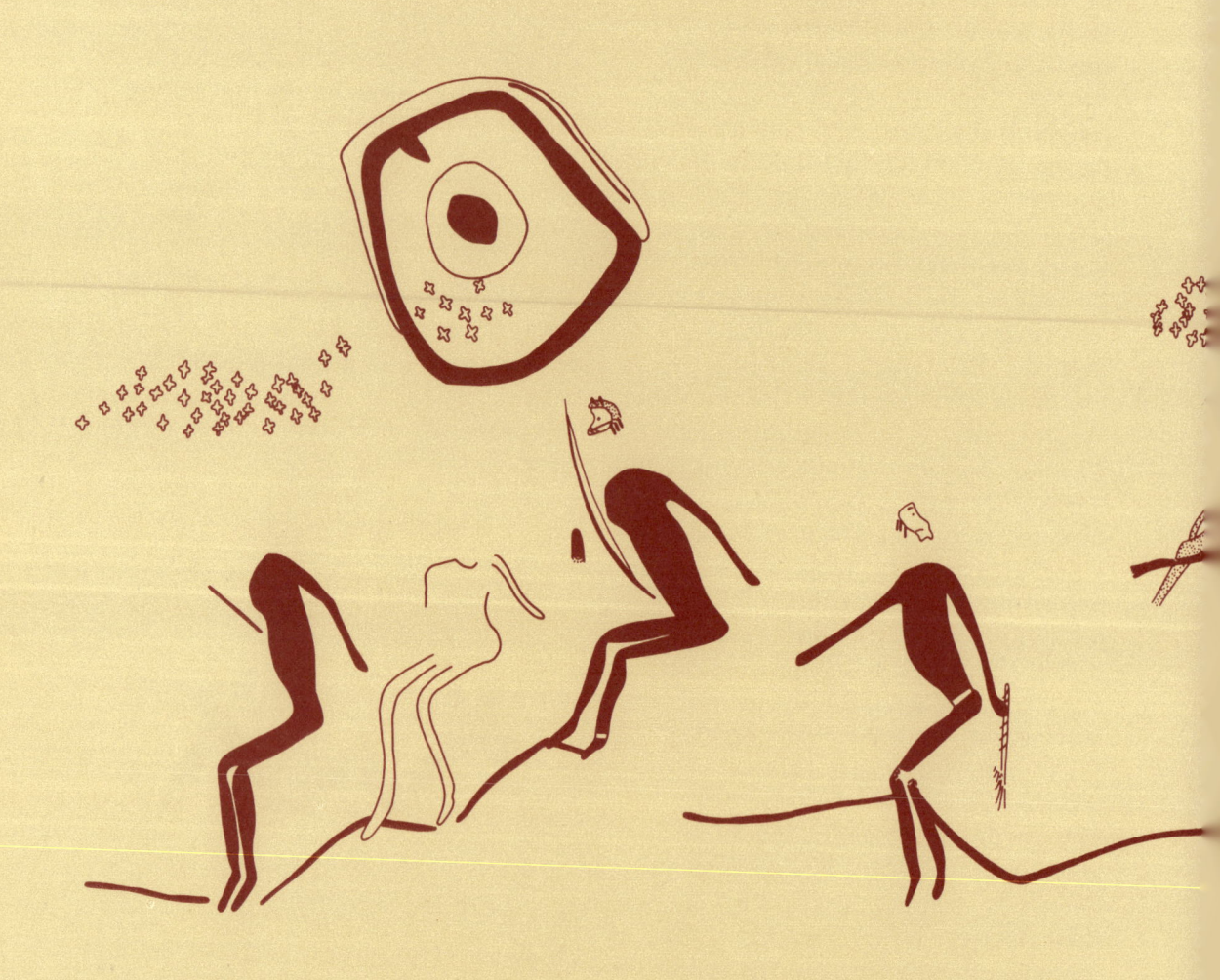

28

Stage III: entoptics and iconics

As people move from the second stage into the third, marked changes in imagery occur. Many laboratory subjects report experiencing a vortex or rotating tunnel, and shamans around the world speak of entering a hole in the ground. The sides of the vortex are marked by a lattice of squares like television screens. The images on these 'screens' are the first spontaneously produced hallucinations of people, animals, houses and other things. They are called *iconic hallucinations*, or simply *iconics*.

The iconic hallucinations of stage three appear to derive from memory and are often associated with powerful emotional experiences. In Western society such images could include knives (for someone who has been assaulted) or an aeroplane (for someone who is afraid of flying). For Bushmen, animals are the most emotionally charged things, and it is therefore not surprising that animals feature prominently in their visions.

Sometimes iconics are integrated with entoptic phenomena that persist into this stage. In Bushman rock art, entoptics and iconics are often combined – just as one would expect to find in depictions of trance experience. This is especially true of the paintings, and it seems that most of the painted entoptics derive from this kind of hallucination.

29. In this painting a grid has been integrated with an eland that has

66

29

large 'tusks' – a still unexplained feature (62). Dots have been scattered throughout the composition, just as the flecks are scattered through other paintings of trance hallucinations or superimposed on paintings of dances (17). But the painting is particularly interesting because, in addition to these features of trance experience, a U-shaped entoptic has been construed as a serpent coming out from beneath a ledge in the rock face (40, 41). It has tusks like those on the eland. Around the eland and the snake there are numerous trance dancers, some of whom are in the distinctive arms-back posture (17). One also has a tusk.

People entering this stage of deep trance report an increase in vividness. They stop using comparisons to describe their experiences and assert that the images are indeed what they appear to be. This painting depicts this vividness in a remarkable way. It brings together all the elements of trance experience established by neuropsychological research: entoptic phenomena are combined with and superimposed on iconic imagery of animals and people; and entoptic forms are construed as things from the shaman's experience. It is, in fact, a classic depiction of hallucinatory experience. Without an understanding of the stages of trance and what people experience in them, this painting would be totally incomprehensible.

TRANCE EXPERIENCE

The third and deepest stage of trance experience is the most complex. All five senses hallucinate in ways that have been established by neuropsychological research, but the manner in which people interpret and react to these hallucinations varies. Each society has its own set of interpretations. If we wish to understand Bushman shamanism, we must therefore bring together the results of neuropsychological research and the specific ways in which Bushmen interpreted and spoke about their hallucinations.

One of the features of deep trance is the blending of different visual hallucinations. Often these are human and animal forms. This experience was described by a Western laboratory subject:

> *I thought of a fox, and instantly I was transformed into that animal. I could distinctly feel myself a fox, could see my long ears and bushy tail, and by a sort of introversion felt that my complete anatomy was that of a fox.*

30, 31. Bushman rock art contains numerous depictions of human beings with animal features that depict just such an experience. These depictions are called *therianthropes*. When, in 1873, J.M. Orpen asked Qing about them (p. 29), the answer he received linked them to the trance dance and used three trance metaphors: 'death' (20, 21), 'underwater' (22), and 'spoilt' (p. 30). Orpen asked specifically about 'men with rhebuck heads', and it is true that most therianthropes combine human and antelope features (30). But human beings are also depicted combined with a range of creatures that includes elephants (31a), baboons (31b) and birds (31c). It seems likely that each kind of therianthrope related to a different – perhaps only slightly different – aspect of trance experience.

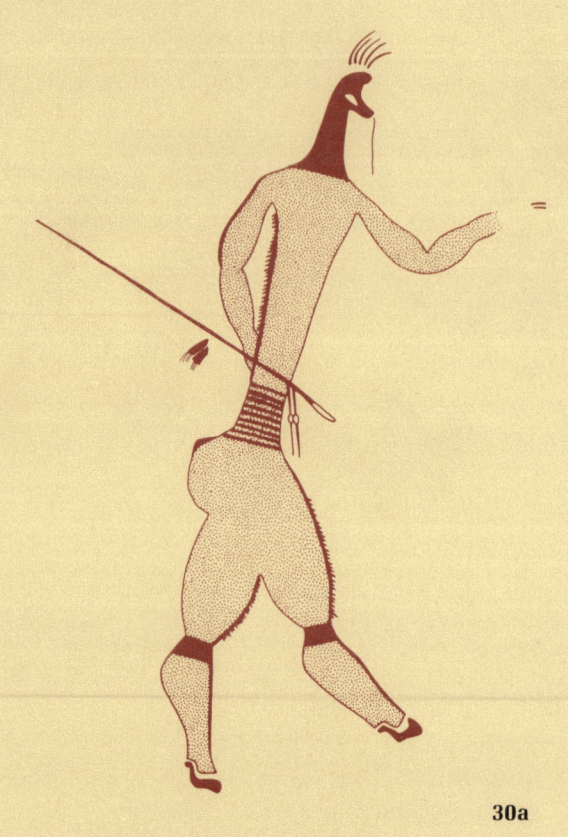

30b

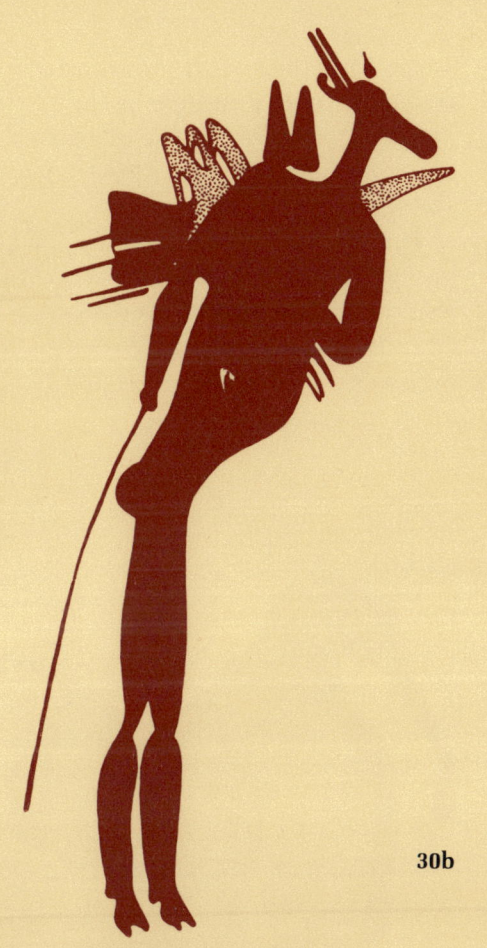

30c

The antelope therianthropes probably reflect a shaman's relationship with the animal from which he derives his potency and after which medicine songs are named. A man may be said to possess, for instance, eland potency, elephant potency or gemsbok potency. This relationship was explained by a /Xam Bushman when Wilhelm Bleek showed him Orpen's copy of a rock painting of antelope therianthropes. Like Qing, he said they were shamans, but he added that they

have things whose bodies they own. These things enable them to appear to see. So it happens that when these things have seen anything which the sorcerer does not know, he perceives by his magic what is happening.

In other words, a shaman who possessed eland power would see what the eland saw and thus know their whereabouts. He could, as it were, slip from one persona to the other. Perhaps, like the Western

69

subject who thought of a fox, Bushman shamans thought of their antelope potency and were 'instantly transformed' into antelope.

The transformation from human to animal identity was accompanied by physical, or *somatic*, hallucinations. One of these was a tingling sensation. Some /Xam people interpreted this as lion's hair growing on the body. They seem to have associated the violent throes of trance with the ferocity of lions (63); people in trance were said to bite other people. To reduce a shaman's frenzy and to remove the 'hair', they rubbed him with fat. This was almost certainly antelope fat. In Bushman thought, antelope and lions are two opposed categories of animal that have a range of symbolic meanings.

Another somatic hallucination seems to be concentrated in certain parts of the body, such as the spine and the waist. Bushmen liken it to the pricking of thorns or arrow points. Kau Dwa, a powerful !Kung shaman, told Katz: 'In your backbone you feel a pointed something and it works its way up. The base of your spine is tingling, tingling, tingling.' In the art, this sensation is represented by small white dots sometimes no bigger than pinheads. They are actually entoptic dots (25) used to depict a physical sensation. This confusion of the senses is common in altered states of consciousness and is called *synaesthesia*; a touch on the skin, for instance, may feel 'blue'. The dots along the spine of the therianthrope in 30c probably represent the 'tingling, tingling' in the shaman's spine as, in his trance experience, he changes into an animal.

The meanings of elephants (66), baboons (64), snakes (62) and birds (65) are explained in the sections dealing with these creatures.

31a

31b

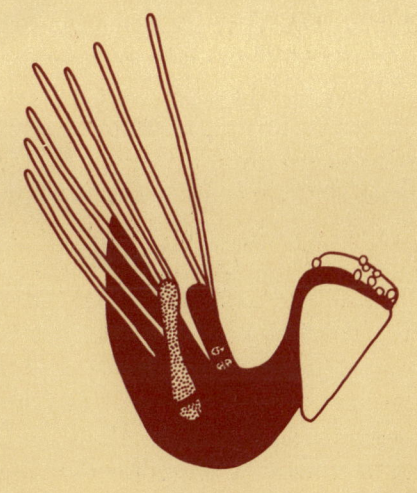

31c

32. A distinctive kind of therianthrope is the *trance-buck*. These paintings, of which the Mlambonja creature (1) is an example, seem to occur only in the southeastern mountains. They depict human figures with features that may include nasal blood (15), antelope heads and hoofs (30), arms in the backward position (17), hairs (20, 30), lines from the top of the head (33), and trailing streamers. Sometimes they hold flywhisks (16d). Often they are in a kneeling posture that recalls the position into which some dancers fall when they enter trance. The trailing streamers probably represent potency entering the shaman's body rather than sickness leaving it. Many trance-buck are in the arms-back posture, and a !Kung man denied that shamans expel sickness in this position. Potency can be seen only by people in trance.

The streamers and the arm position of some examples give the impression that they are flying, but others are more probably kneeling on the ground. There appears to be a continuum from standing and perhaps bending-forward therianthropes to kneeling figures with the heels shown, to fully formed trance-buck that appear to have no legs at all.

32a

The wide variety within what is clearly a category of painting (no engraved examples of trance-buck are known) may be attributed to the idiosyncratic nature of Bushman religion. Because each trance-buck represents a shaman's hallucination, each is a unique variation on a theme. Each is, in fact, a shaman's personal, idiosyncratic revelation of the spirit world and what happens to those who enter it.

32b

32c

32d

Trance-buck (32a, b) and other figures often have long lines emanating from the top of the head. In some instances, **33a**, these lines may depict feathers stuck in the hair or in a band around the head, but in many cases, **33b**, the lines are so long as to defy any naturalistic interpretation. These long examples of the lines more probably derive from trance experience, as do so many other non-realistic features of the art.

The explanation for this feature again lies in a combination of neuropsychological evidence and

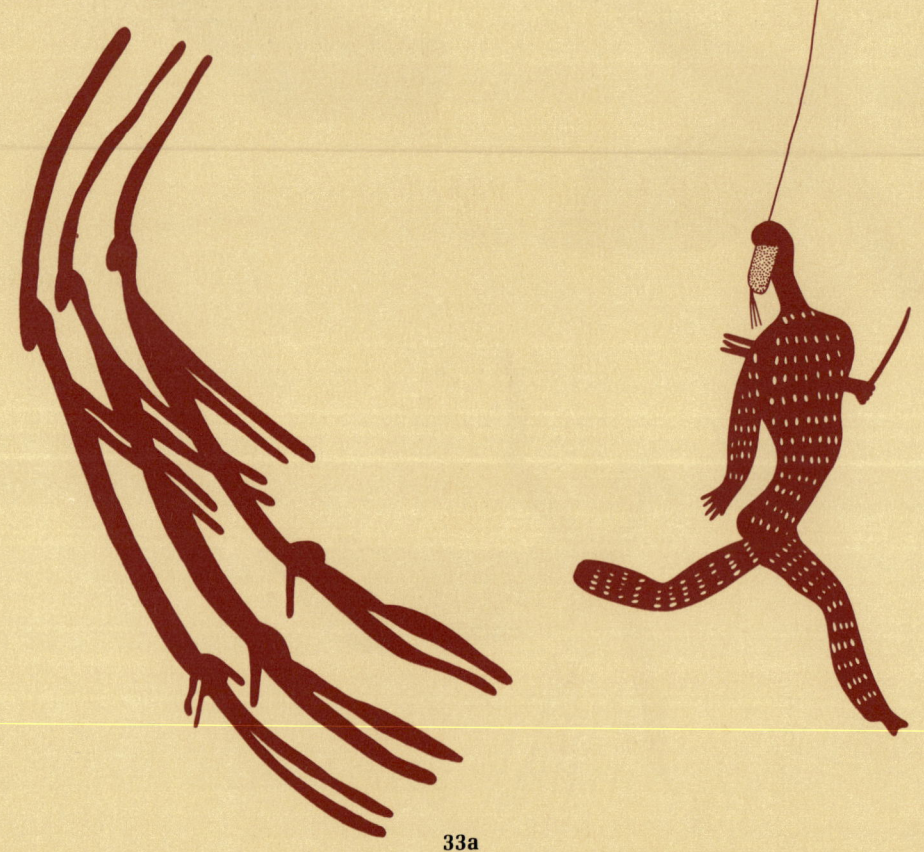

33a

33b

Bushman beliefs. Laboratory research has shown that people in certain states of altered consciousness experience a tingling sensation in the top of the head. Schizophrenia, which has much in common with trance experience, sometimes produces a similar feeling. One patient described it as a fish hook in his scalp being drawn upwards.

This sensation may have been the basis for the Bushman belief that, when a trancer's spirit leaves his body, it does so through a 'hole' in the top of the head. The departing spirit can be seen only by other shamans. The lines leaving the heads of many human figures therefore probably represent the spirit leaving on out-of-body travel.

33c. Some paintings have what at first glance may appear to be high, pointed caps, but which more probably depict the sensation described by the schizophrenia patient. These paintings depict somatic hallucinations.

These lines and pointed heads again suggest that the paintings of which they are part, no matter what realistic components they may have, actually depict a shaman's view of the interaction between this world and the spirit world.

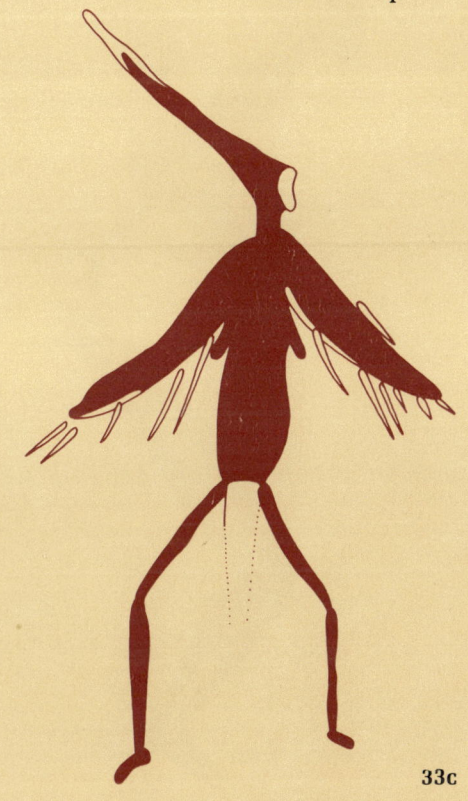

33c

Elongated human figures are a common feature of Bushman rock art in all parts of the subcontinent. Their elongation has been interpreted as a stylistic feature of the art and as an attempt on the part of a diminutive people to represent themselves as tall. Writers have also tried to distinguish the elongated figures on the grounds of race and to propose the intrusion of mysterious tall people into the Bushmen's traditional areas. All these interpretations go counter to the way in which Bushman rock art should be understood. They see the art from a Western point of view and assume that the meaning of the art can be simply inferred from the art itself (p. 23-26). By now it has become clear that this approach is doomed to failure.

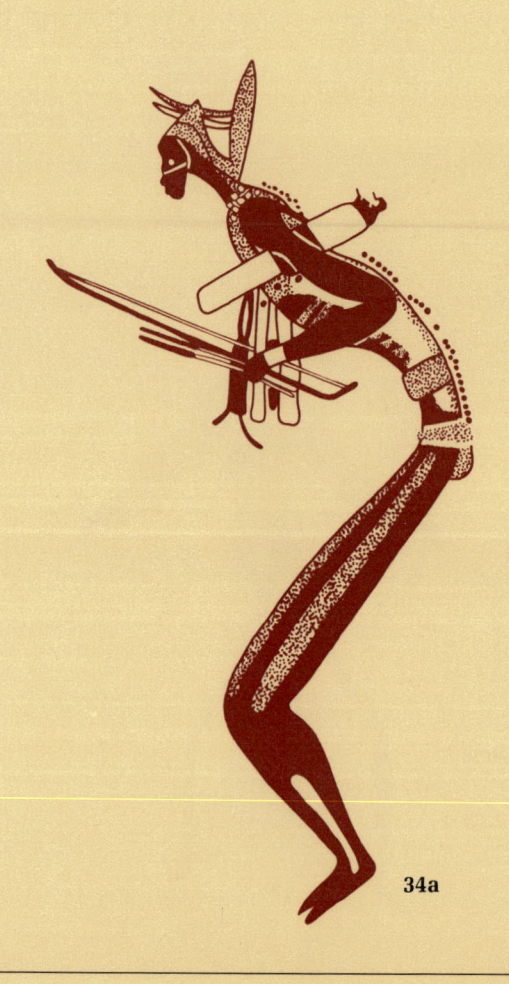

34a

To explain the elongation of human figures in Bushman rock art, we turn to another commonly reported physical hallucination. As we have seen, Bushman shamans speak of the potency in their stomachs beginning to rise up the spine until it 'explodes' in the head. This sensation increases until they experience a sense of attenuation in their limbs and body. One !Kung man pointed to a tree and said that he was as tall as that when he was in trance.

The elongated dancer in **34a** is particularly interesting. It has a strange 'headdress' that is probably an elaborated depiction of the sensation felt in the top of the head (33), and a line of dots along its spine. As with the therianthropes in 30c, these dots probably represent the man's rising potency and are, again like 30c, related to his attenuation.

34b. In what is perhaps the most striking depiction of attenuation, three human figures extend down the rock face for 67 cm. Each is in a trancing posture. The first from the left has its hands on its chest in an oft-repeated posture that may be related to the tingling sensation experienced in a person's 'front spine', as Bushmen call the sternum. The next figure has its hands up in a familiar dancing posture (16b), and the last one is in the arms-back posture (17). All three are clearly trance dancers.

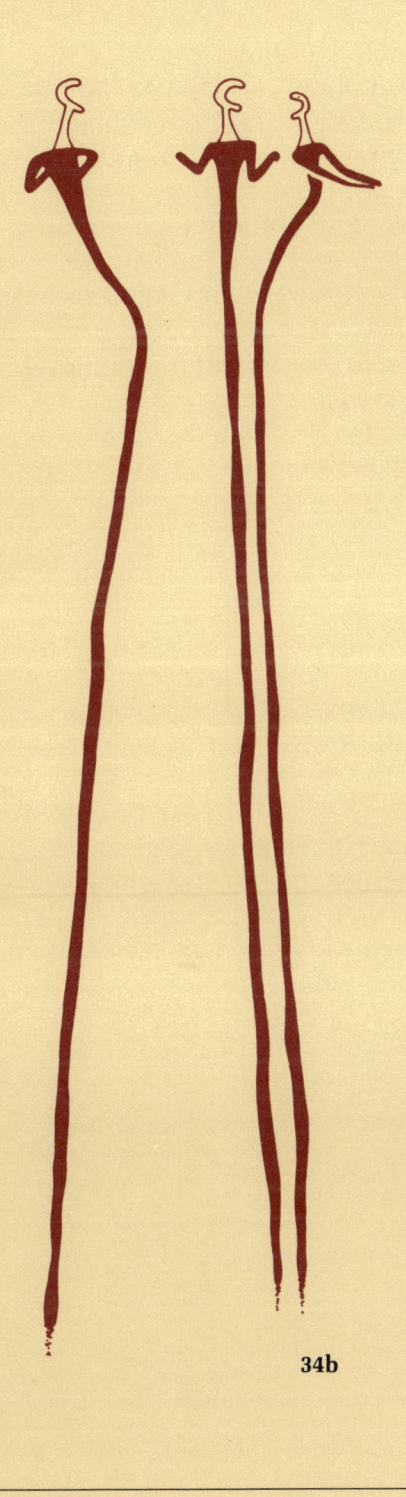

34b

77

Another curious feature of Bushman rock art is extra limbs and digits. At one time it was thought that the artist could not make up his or her mind on just how, for instance, to represent the legs of an antelope and ended up with one too many. There are, however, reasons for questioning this conclusion.

One of the therianthropes in **35a** has an extra finger. Trance blood falls from its nose (15). On the accompanying figure there are also zigzags and dots that could possibly have been attributed to body paint were it not for the fact that they trail off the leg and become small heart-shapes similar to the larger ones on the 'objects' they appear to hold. The body marks are more probably entoptic dots and zigzags (25, 26) that, by synaesthesia (30, 31), confuse visual hallucinations with physical experience. These therianthropes are therefore complex depictions of trance experience, and the extra finger should be considered part of that experience.

Research has shown that *polymelia*, the hallucination of having extra digits and limbs, is fairly common in certain altered states and is a better explanation for this feature than error or indecision. In fact, the extra limbs possessed by numerous depictions of animals are carefully drawn and clearly intentional (**35b**, 24).

In **35c**, the standing figure has an extra arm that seems to have been created by overpainting a white figure so that one arm of the original figure is preserved. Next to this figure, the small dog-like creature with erect hair (20, 30, 31, 32) has two extra legs. The juxtaposition of these two paintings raises the question of whether animals are really shamans in animal form.

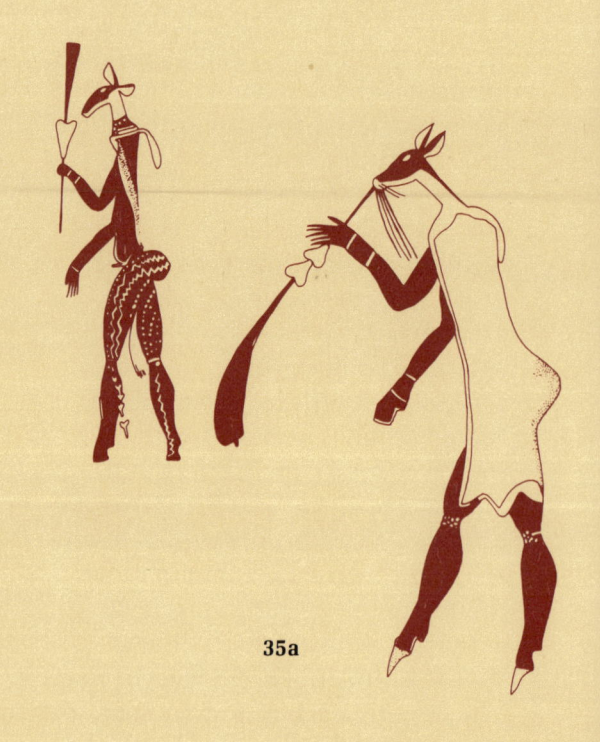

35a

35b

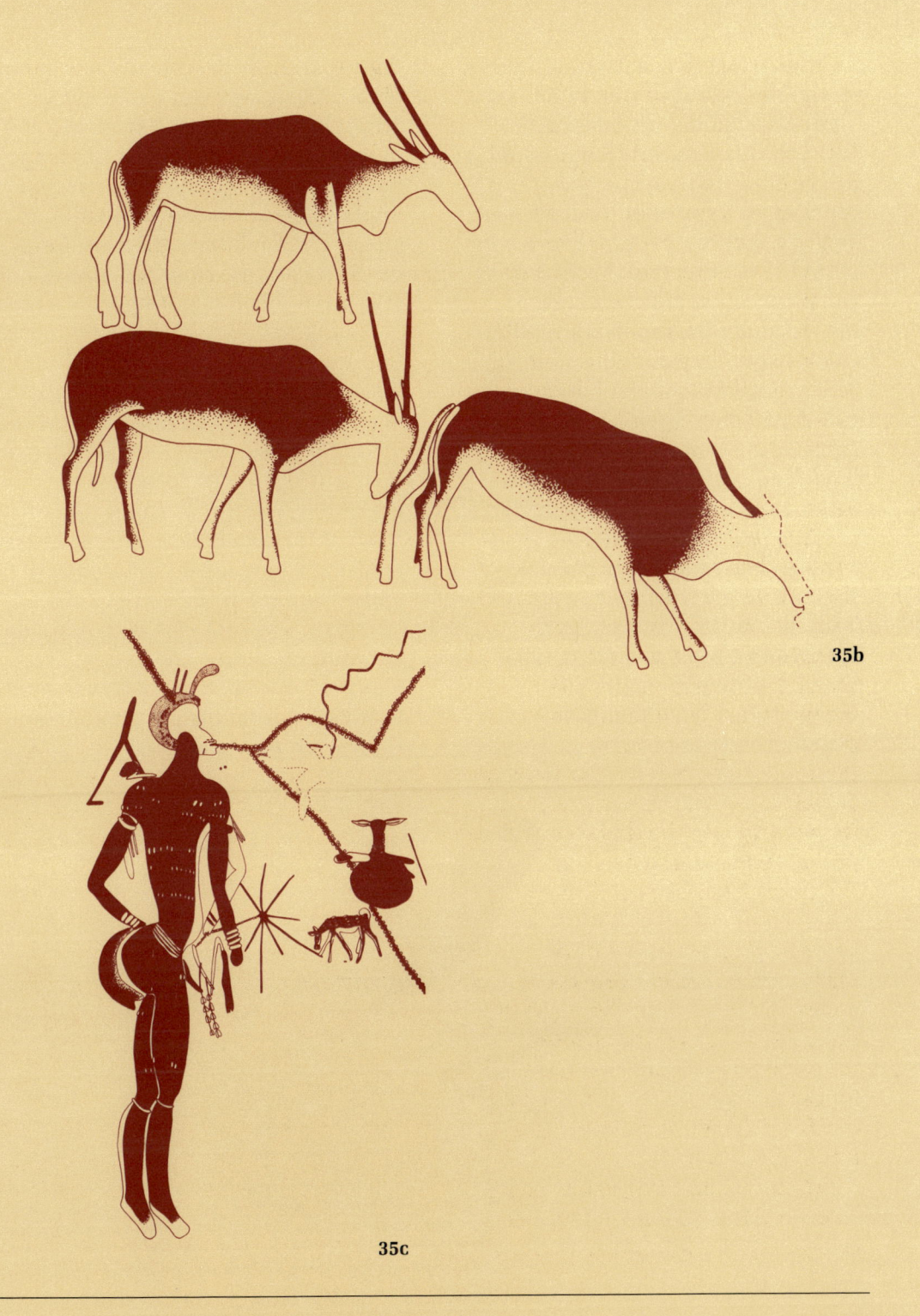

35c

Close inspection of human figures sometimes reveals a number of very finely drawn lines on their faces. Often the lines radiate from a spot where, more or less, one would suppose the nose to be. Sometimes they are vertical. People who see the art as literal interpret these lines as scarifications or tattoo marks.

36a. To show the problems with this literal view, we examine a painting which, unlike most (49c), has a nose, mouth and chin. In this case, the facial lines clearly radiate from the nose. Next, **36b**, we look at a figure with raised knee (19c) that has facial lines *and* trance blood falling from its nose. The connection between nasal blood and facial lines was explained by the old southern Bushwoman interviewed in 1985 (p. 36). Bending forward, she demonstrated how Bushman shamans had danced when she was young, and she described their nasal blood. Then, when she was asked what the shamans did with the blood, she drew her hands across her face, showing they had smeared it back exactly how the painted lines suggest. Facial lines are, therefore, probably another and sometimes stylised way of depicting trance blood.

An interesting development of this feature is that facial lines sometimes also appear on animals, especially eland. They can be easily overlooked. The example in **36c** also has two heads (35), an effect that has been created by careful overpainting of most of the recumbent animal and by creating a new head that seems to share the ears of the earlier painted antelope. The fact that both animals and human beings have facial lines is another pointer to the conclusion that many animals may be shamans in their animal personae.

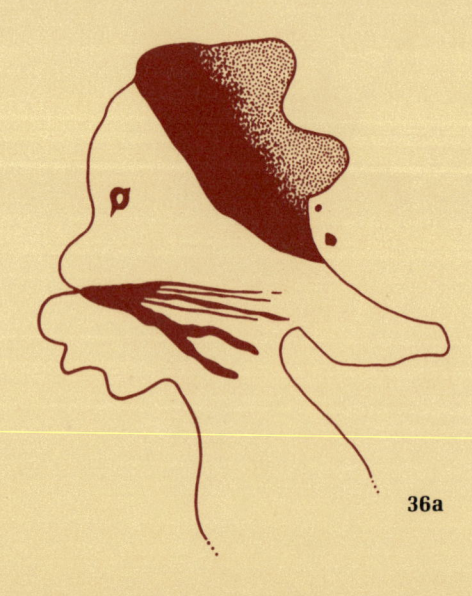

36a

36b

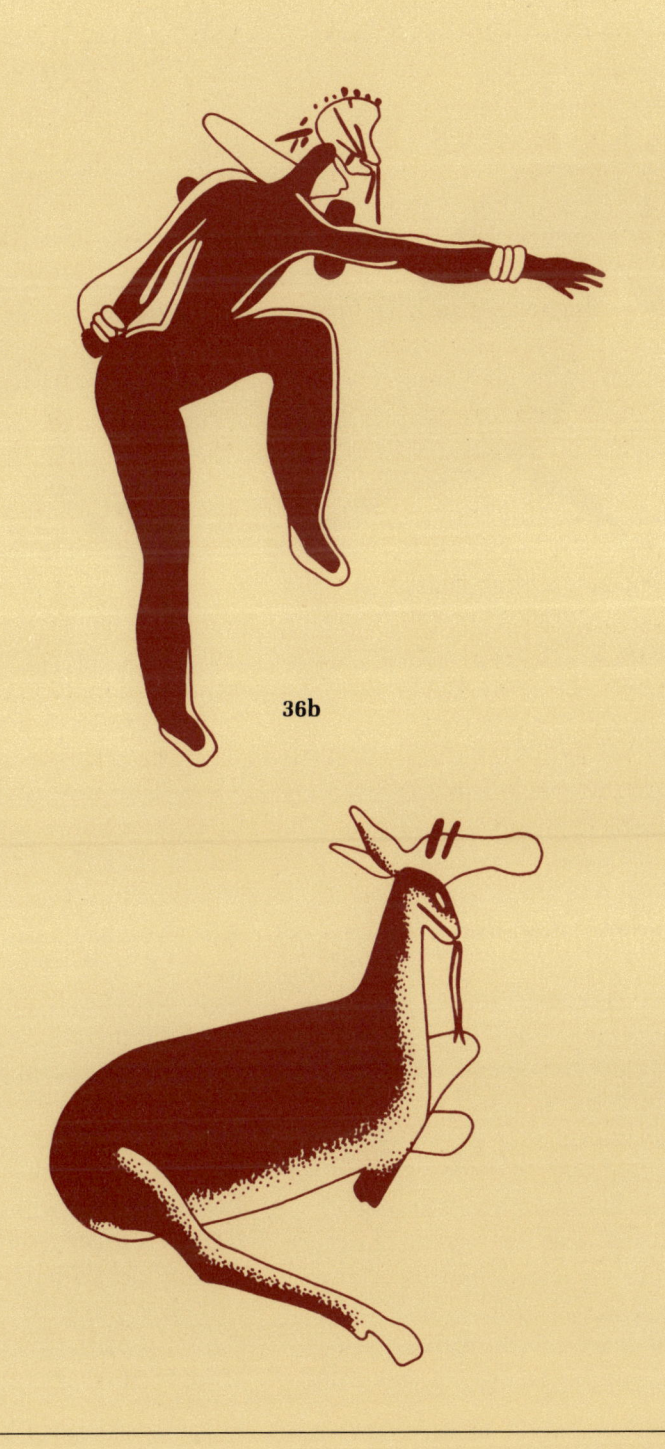

36c

37a.

Extra limbs (35) and facial lines (36) are not the only unusual features found in some depictions of animals. Sometimes animal bodies are distorted in other ways, each of which must have had some significance for the artists.
37a. So far we have seen paintings that combine human and animal features. Sometimes a painting combines features of different animal species. In this example, horse (70) and eland features are mixed. Like all the other curious features of the art, this combination was not just a whimsical fancy. Even though we cannot be sure of the exact meaning of such a depiction, there can be little doubt that the artist wanted to say something specific.
37b. An association between horns and the long lines that issue from the tops of some trancers' heads (33) is suggested by a painting that shows a dancing man and a 'dancing' eland. The eland has elongated horns, and the man, the top part of whose body is painted to echo the eland, has a long line extending upwards. This dancer with raised knee (19c) is accompanied by his eland potency or, more possibly, the eland *is* a dancing shaman thoroughly transformed by eland potency.

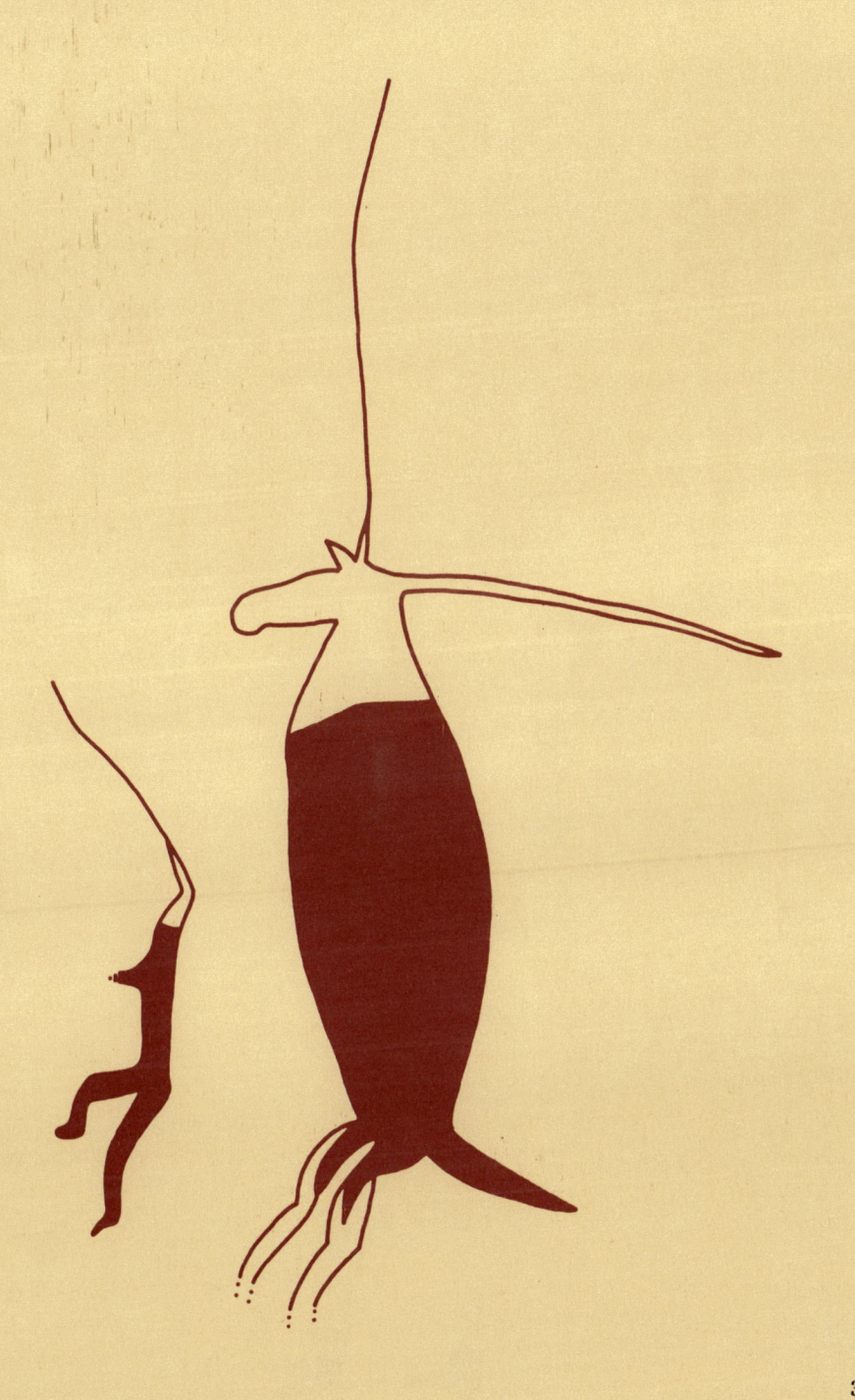

37b

38. All the beliefs and painted features we have described give an idea, however faint, of what Bushman shamans experienced in trance. But some paintings are so detailed that they provide unusual insights into the hallucinatory world. The three figures shown here are from a long line of very complexly painted shamans and give us some understanding of the variety and detail of the shaman-artists' visions. These paintings are particularly well preserved because they have been in the Africana Museum, Johannesburg, for many years.

The legs of the figures are covered with grid and zigzag patterns which, like many others (35a), are probably entoptic (26). Two figures (38a) hold aloft antelope forelegs with cloven hoofs.

38a

84

38b

Even more interesting is the figure with the 'bird' perched on its head (38b). The 'bird' has long streamers that recall those of some trance-buck (32). It is probably the man's spirit in the form of a bird and therefore a different version of the long lines leaving the top of some figures' heads (33). This figure's head has antelope ears, a curious 'tusk', an open mouth with teeth, and two facial lines (36). It is another combination of different animal species to produce a 'monster' or chimera.

Metaphors (20-24) and transformations (30-41) are the essence of trance experience. But metaphors and transformations also interact with one another to produce new and sometimes unique depictions. In **39a**, two trancers bleed from the nose (15). The accompanying bird and fish refer to the flight (23) and underwater (22) metaphors of trance experience. The nasal blood is, in some sense, 'literal' because it can be seen by anyone at a trance dance, but the bird and the fish are 'metaphorical' because they refer, by comparison with animals, to states not accessible to ordinary people.

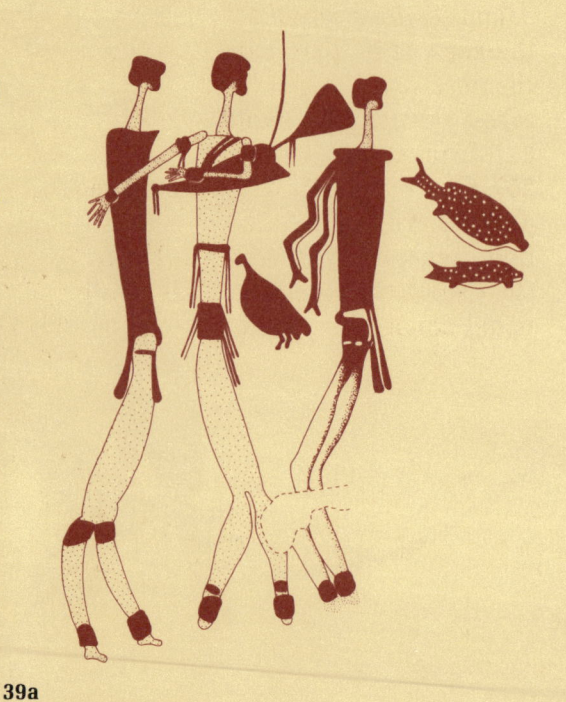

39a

The most interesting feature of the painting is the way the artist has taken the underwater metaphor a stage further than usual and used it in a transformation: one of the figures has arms that end in fishtails. He is part terrestrial man, and part aquatic fish. In other words, he spans two worlds – this world and the spirit world that people enter by going underwater. This is the only fish-man so far discovered in this region. It is therefore a new idea about religious belief and experience put forward by a shaman-artist. Moreover, the figure's arms are zigzags. (p. 35, 67a).

86

39b. Paintings of figures with zigzag legs are known, and when Katz asked !Kung shamans to draw themselves as they conceived of themselves, they produced various forms derived, by synaesthesia (30, 31), from entoptic phenomena (25, 26). One man, **39c**, drew zigzag legs and a zigzag spine. The rest of his body was, he said, represented by the detached zigzags. In trance all usual constraints vanish.

39b

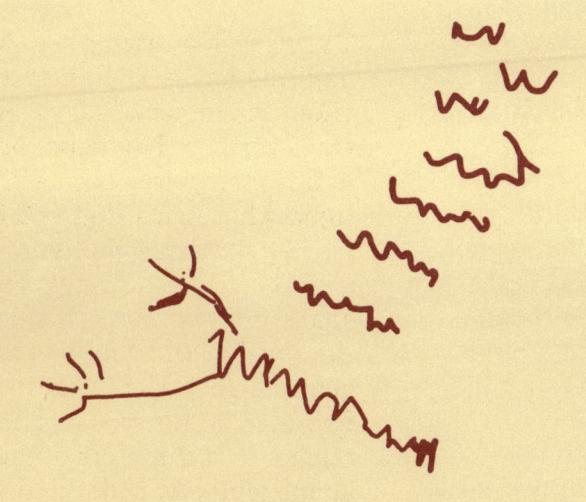

39c

Bushman shamans often speak of travelling underground, a journey that frequently starts by diving into a waterhole (22). This concept appears in the art in a very literal way.

In **40**, there is a deep groove or fold in the rock face around which an artist has applied black paint. Two therianthropes (30, 31) and a number of other figures, one of whom bleeds from the nose (15), rise up (or sink into) the black paint and the groove. Around them there are eight fish, two eels, two turtles and a large number of flywhisks (16d). All these depictions add up to 'underwater' trance experience (22) and, more specifically, entrance into a waterhole or pool. The idea is developed in the upper left part of the group where another black area – but this time not associated with a deep groove – has four fishtails protruding from it, and, down left also, where a second black area has two more therianthropes coming out of it.

Many other paintings show animals, often serpents with antelope heads (29, 47b, 62), coming from cracks or steps in the rock. One very large example of a serpent passes, as it were, behind a large boss of rock and reappears on the other side. In other instances, paintings have been carefully painted in hollows in the rock face.

40

One of the most interesting features of Bushman rock art is a red line often fringed with tiny white dots. It seems to perform various functions. Sometimes it is at the feet of human figures as if it were a dancing rut (14, 28). In other paintings, **41a**, it links depictions by apparently passing in and out of animals and human beings or by forming a kind of 'path'. Often it branches and weaves its way across a couple of metres of rock face, entering and leaving at cracks, steps and angles.

The example shown in **41b** is particularly interesting because it is unusually compact and all ends of the line are preserved. All too often only portions are preserved. Four branches of the line emerge from (or enter into) a 3 mm groove in the rock. Three of these branches each end at a very small, hardly noticeable step in the rock face varying from 2 to 4 mm. One simply ends on a smooth area. The lower branch is closely associated with a human figure in the kneeling, arms-back posture adopted by trance-buck (32). It has 'hairs' along its arms that seem to echo the dots on the line. This figure and the line are superimposed (72-73) on an eland.

Possible explanations for the line include supernatural potency and the trajectory of a shaman on out-of-body travel. But, for the present, its most interesting feature is the way it weaves in and out of the rock face. On this side of the rock it is associated with paintings. What happens to it when it is on the other, for us invisible, side of the rock? Perhaps there, too, it is associated with 'paintings'.

41a

41b

    This line and the other paintings that enter and leave the rock face (29, 40, 47b) suggest that, for the shaman-artists, the spirit world lay behind the wall of the rock shelter. Perhaps the rock shelter was the entrance to the spirit world. The shamans reached through the wall, extracted the beings and events of the spirit world, and then fixed them on the rock for all to see. If this is so, the paintings are not paintings as we normally understand the word. For the Bushmen, many of them may have been the actual contents of the spirit world made visible first by the shamans' hallucinations and then by the shaman-artists' skill.

RAIN-MAKING

One of the Bushman shamans' most important tasks was to make rain. Orpen and Bleek discovered, quite independently, exactly how they did this. Orpen learned about rain-making when Qing took him to a painting depicting the procedure, and Bleek was told about it when he showed Orpen's copy of the painting to the people who were living with him in Cape Town. Subsequently, Bleek's informants commented on copies of other paintings of rain-making. The meaning of these paintings is thus particularly well attested.

The southern Bushmen thought of the rain as an animal. Generally, it was a rather amorphous quadruped that in some ways resembled a hippopotamus, but it could also look like an antelope or an ox. In a /Xam myth, an eland actually *is* the rain. The Bushmen called this creature *!khwa-ka xoro*, the rain's animal. A male rain-animal, or rain-bull, was associated with the frightening thunderstorms that bellowed, stirred up the dust, and sometimes killed people with its lightning. The female rain-animal was associated with soft, soaking rains. Columns of rain falling from a storm cloud were called 'the rain's legs', and the soft wisps under the clouds were 'the rain's hair'. We should not, however, suppose that the Bushmen thought a rain cloud *was* an animal. A Bushman told Bleek that the rain's

42

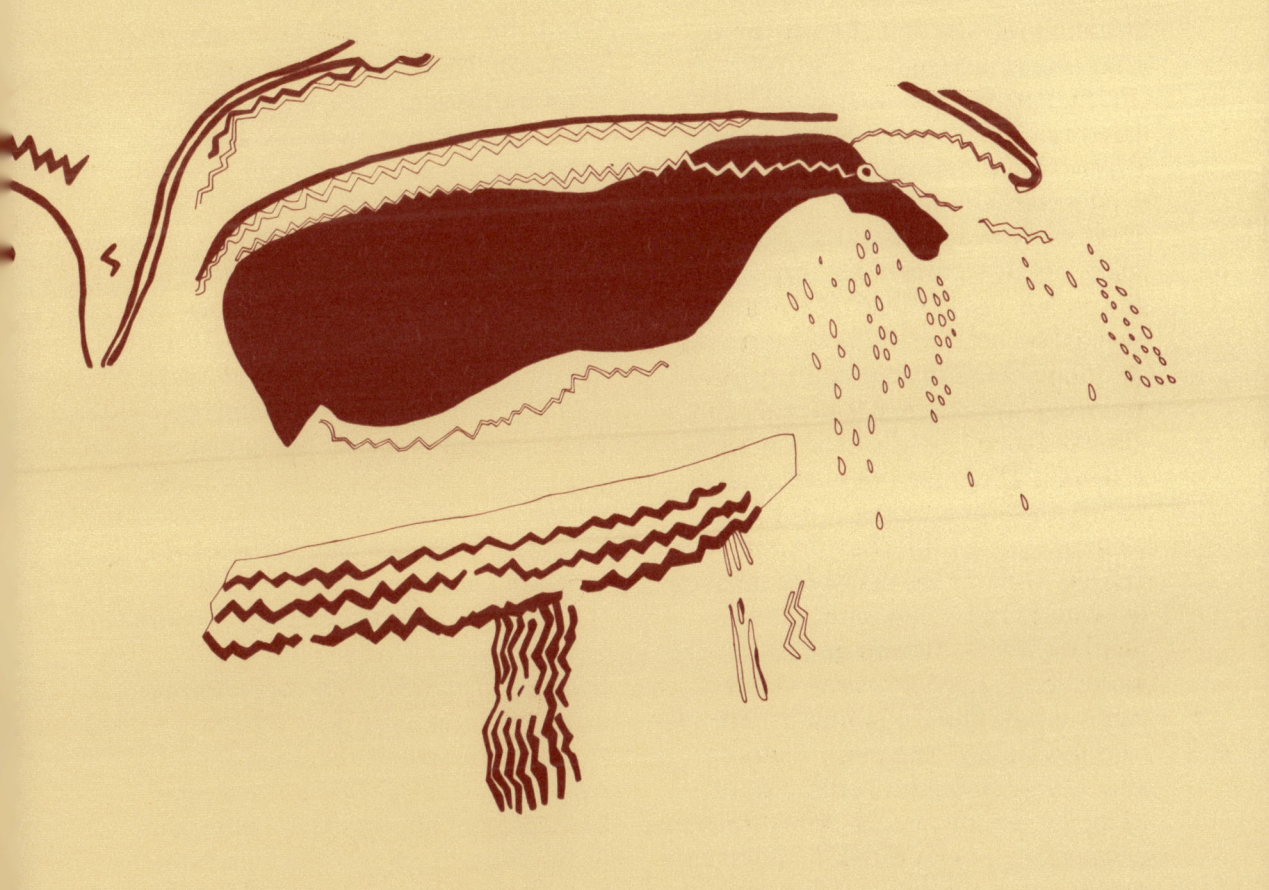

legs were actually the rain streaming down. Like the English 'raining cats and dogs', it was, at least in some usages, simply a way of speaking.

But the rain-animal also appeared in shamans' hallucinations and, in this context, was probably more 'real' and not just a figure of speech. When rain was urgently needed, people approached the shamans of the rain (!khwa-ka !gi:ten) and asked them to cause it to rain. The shamans then entered trance, probably at a trance dance, though they could also make rain by 'dreaming'. In the spirit world, they tried to capture a rain-animal. Qing, discussing a painting of the capture of the rain-animal, said the shamans were underwater (22), that they had been 'spoilt by the dance' (p. 29), and that 'their noses bleed' (15). In other words, he believed that the rain-making shamans depicted in the painting had entered trance at a trance dance.

Bleek's /Xam people gave additional information. They said the shamans of the rain caught the rain-animal at night by throwing a thong over its horns as it came out of a pool. This was a dangerous undertaking, and a fierce rain-bull could break the thong and escape. To calm an 'angry' rain-bull, a young girl sprinkled *buchu* (an aromatic herb) on the surface of the waterhole because, as one of Bleek's informants put it, 'the rain loves buchu very much. It glides quietly along when it smells things which are unequalled in scent.' In Bushman thought, scent is closely associated with supernatural potency.

When they had captured a rain-animal, the shamans of the rain led it across the parched veld and killed it. Its blood and milk then became rain. Sometimes they 'rode' it to the top of a mountain and killed it there so that the rain would run down the mountain slopes. At other times they cooked the animal's meat and threw 'it away on the places where they want the rain to fall'. Although, on occasion, these rituals may have been performed with a real animal, such as an eland or an ox, the accounts show that the rain-animal was usually part of trance experience, in other words, a hallucination.

In the art, rain-making scenes are very varied. In **42**, two animals are surrounded by zigzags and dots. It seems likely that these geometric forms depict entoptic phenomena (25-26). In stage III hallucinations, animals are often combined with entoptics (29). We cannot be sure that the shaman-artists thought of the zigzags as a pool, clouds or rain because the tail of the left-hand animal turns into a zigzag, another zigzag merges with and passes through the eye of the animal on the right and, finally, this animal also has a zigzag apparently coming out of its body. It seems more probable that the zigzags represent the rain's potency. The rain was, in fact, considered to be very powerful indeed. Because of its power, newly fallen rain had to be respected. In any event, the combination of animals with geometrics is clearly a stage III hallucination.

In **43**, zigzags and dots are again associated with a rain-animal, but here the dots run along the animal's spine (30c, 34a). Zigzags are also associated with the numerous therianthropes surrounding the animal.

Less transformed people are chasing a rain-animal in **44**. Some of them have geometric patterns on their bodies (25-26).

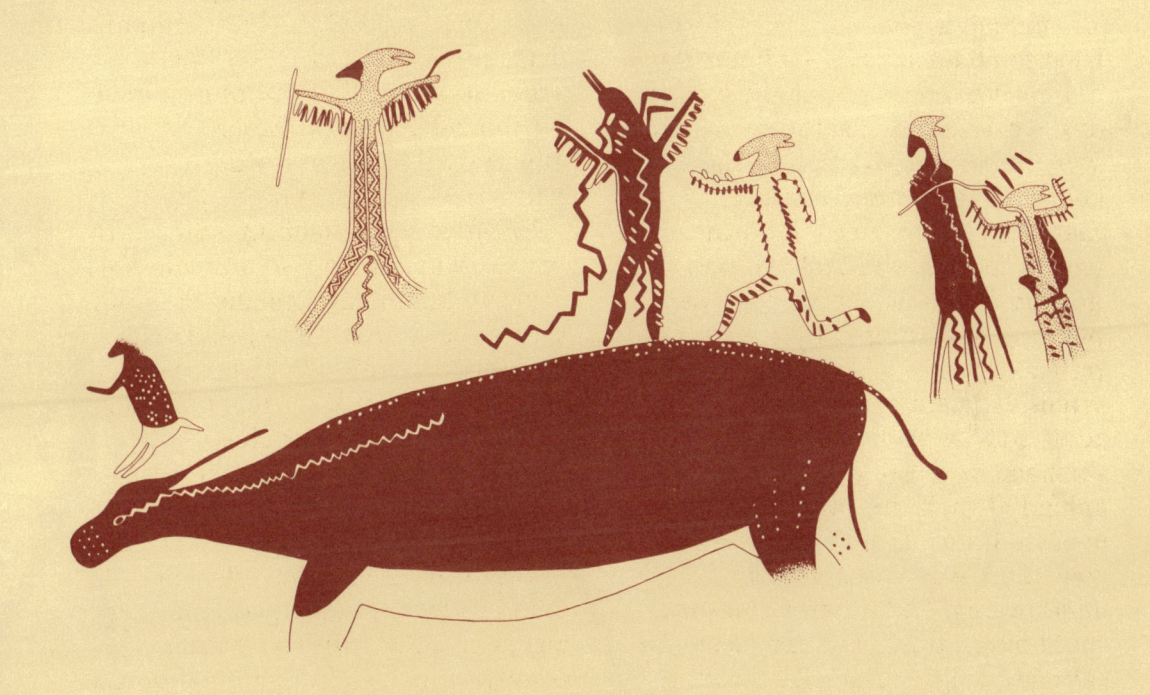

43

96

44

Where they kill the rain-bull,
There the rain runs along the ground.
Then the wild onion leaves sprout
   for the people,
And they dig and feed themselves
   with them.
Then the people who are at home see
   the rain clouds
And they say to each other,
'The medicine men really seem to
   have their hands upon the
   rain-bull,
For you to see the rain clouds come
   gliding.'
      Wilhelm Bleek's informant
      Diä!kwain
          1874

45

CONTROL OF ANIMALS

Another of the shamans' tasks was to ensure good hunting by controlling the movements of antelope herds. These were the shamans of the game who were said to 'possess' antelope.

Wilhelm Bleek's informants spoke of shamans of the game wearing caps made from springbok scalps and sewn so that the ears stood up. One of these people was a woman named Tãnõ-khauken. The second part of her name means 'tremble', and the word was also used to describe shamans trembling in trance. She was said to 'possess' springbok. She also claimed to have a springbok which she kept tied up and which she sent among the wild springbok so that it would lead the herd towards the place where she lived. She referred to this animal as her 'heart's springbok'. It was, she said, 'not a food springbok'. Because of these two remarks and because it seems most unlikely that a springbok could be trained to act as a decoy, this animal was probably, like the rain-animal (42-44), hallucinatory. It existed in the spirit rather than the real world.

Tãnõ-khauken also claimed that a man had killed her 'heart's springbok'. Another man who had eaten some of it was taken ill, but she said she would not 'take this person away'. She was mollified when the mother of Bleek's informant made an eared cap out of the springbok and gave it to her. In return she gave the woman her old cap: 'Take my old cap, keep it and see whether the springbok do not follow the cap to where it goes.' Accounts like this show just how closely the real and the spirit world were interrelated.

In the art, eared caps are quite common. They are usually distinguishable from the antelope heads of therianthropes; the cap rests on a normal human head. The ears are often very carefully drawn, with the inside of the ears a darker colour. This is true of the cap worn by the man in **46**. Even though the painting is very small, it is drawn in great detail. He is also wearing a kaross over which he has slung a quiver. The arrow in the bow has what appears to be a triangular metal point. Bushmen obtained iron from black farmers (68-69); today Bushmen fashion points from fencing wire. The other arrows have slender bone points (52). The hunter holds one of these in readiness so that, as soon as the arrow in the bow has been discharged, the second can be brought down swiftly. The remaining three arrows are lodged between his body and the kaross. Hunters also kept arrows in arm, head and waist bands to facilitate rapid shooting. That this man is seated suggests he is waiting in ambush for a herd to run past.

The bow-string, painted in white, connects to the lower extremity of the stave and to a point a little distance from the upper end. This is because the string is permanently attached to one end of the stave, while the other end of the string is a loop that is hooked over the stave and slid down until it lodges. When not in use, bows are kept unstrung.

Much of the painting is thus detailed and 'realistic'. There are, however, white dots on the man's legs, as there are on some rain-animals (43) and therianthropes (30c). Because such dots are probably entoptic (25), it is more than likely that this man is hunting in the spirit realm. A Kalahari man said that he had actually killed an eland while hunting in trance. The next day, he claimed, he had taken his family to the carcass and they had feasted.

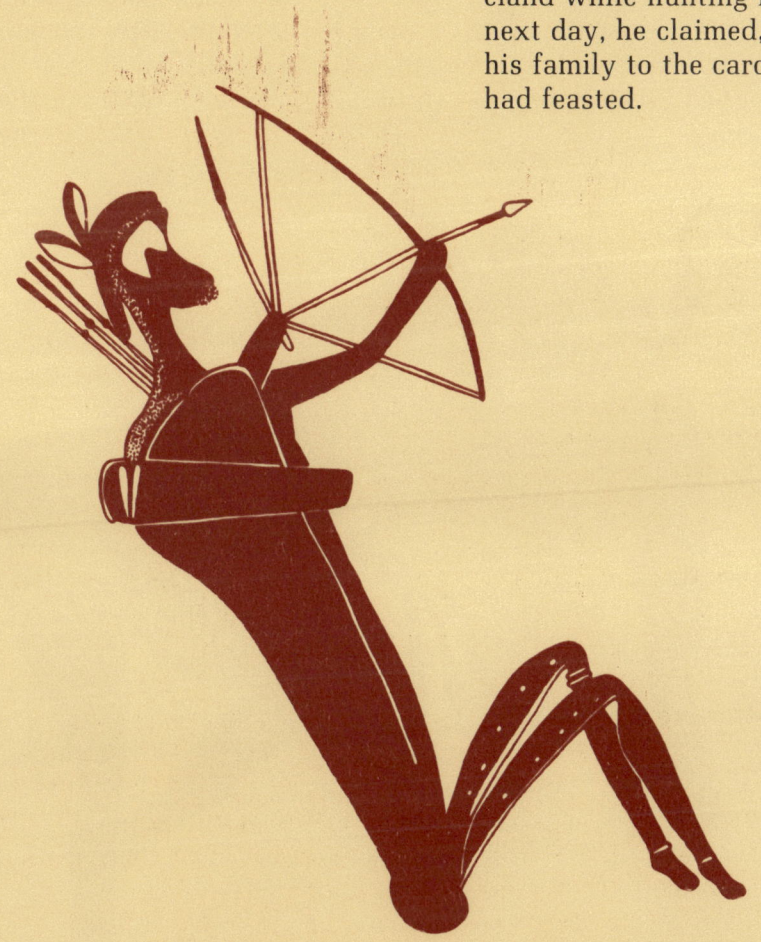

46

Other suggestions in the art of supernatural control of animals have not yet been confirmed by Bushman statements or explanations. One of these hints is the antelope legs in **47a** that human figures sometimes hold. Usually they appear to be forelegs. Sometimes the legs are not held but are simply painted in sets. Another painted feature that may be related to the legs and, thus, to control, is hoofprints (**47b**, 75). Often these are so clearly painted and engraved that one can hazard a good guess at the species of antelope represented. In one painting a large therianthrope leaves black hoofprints trailing for over a metre behind him. A Kalahari Bushman identified the spoor as that of eland. Sometimes it is even possible to tell that the animal is near to death because the two parts of the print are splayed out.

A clue as to the meaning of these paintings may come from first-kill rituals (p. 118-119). After a boy has killed his first large antelope, preferably an eland, he is scarified

47a

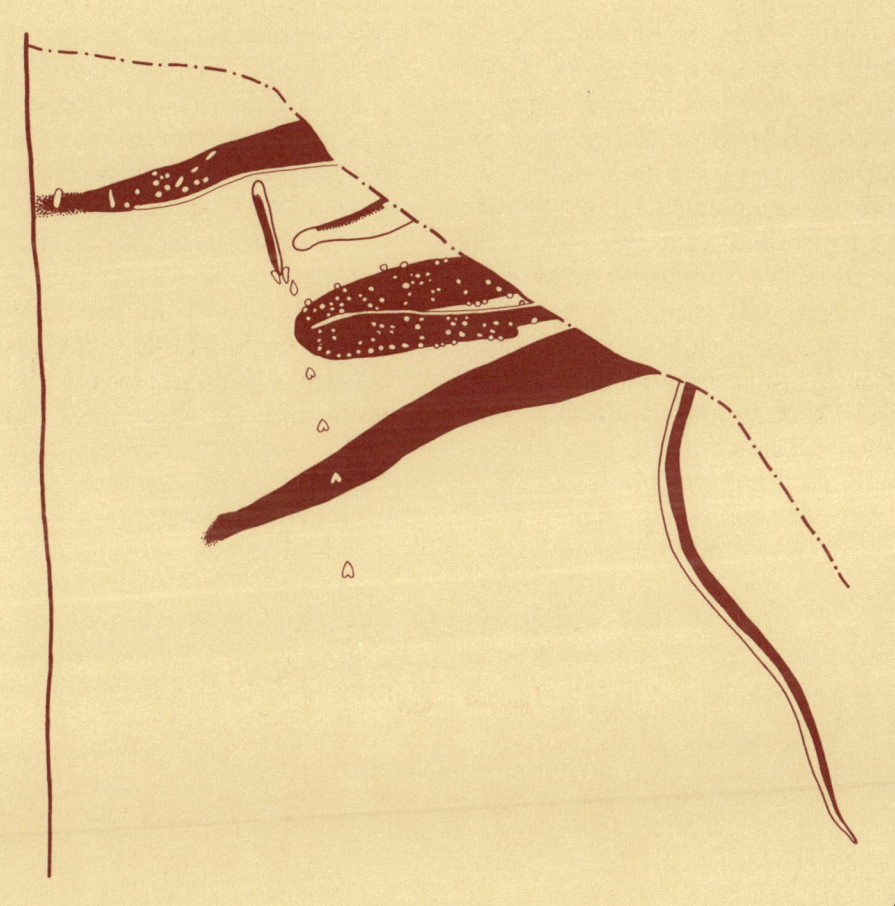

47b

and various rituals are performed. At one point he sits on the antelope skin while a man uses one of the eland's forelegs, left if it is a female, right if it is a male, to make a circle of hoofprints around the skin. They say that, as the boy has to cross these prints when he rises and leaves the skin, so, in life, he will come across eland spoor and be a successful hunter. The depictions of antelope legs and spoor may imply that shamans of the game possessed antelope legs and that they could use these to control the movements of herds by laying down a track for the animals to follow in the same way that herds were said to follow the wearer of an eared cap or a 'pet' springbok that was usually kept tied up.

THE HUMAN FIGURE

It is often said that Bushman art depicts many hunting scenes. In fact, comparatively few human figures are shown engaged in hunting. In the Ndedema Gorge in the Natal Drakensberg, Harald Pager identified only 29 hunting scenes among 3 909 individual paintings. Of these 29 hunting scenes, merely seven show men actually shooting at the game, and only one animal is depicted as having been hit by an arrow. Far more paintings seem to show men simply running after game. Of course, we should remember that the very act of carrying hunting equipment may have implied hunting in this or in the spirit world. A !Kung person, asked where a certain man is, may reply, 'He has put his quiver on' – in other words, he has gone hunting.

The next most frequently depicted activity in the Ndedema Gorge is dancing. There are 13 dance scenes. But we must remember that, for the Bushmen, many other depictions of human beings were associated with dancing by flywhisks (16d) and certain distinctive postures (14-19), even though they are not part of one of these larger 'scenes'. It is, in fact, impossible to categorise depictions of people as 'standing', 'walking', 'running' or 'sitting' simply by noting the positions of their legs; numerous other features must be taken into account. Many of the inventories of paintings and engravings that have been compiled with great care and labour are unfortunately flawed because the researchers who compiled them were unaware of these significant features. Nevertheless, despite all these problems, the general impression given by the Drakensberg paintings is one of activity and liveliness; this is less so in the western Cape and some of the areas where engravings predominate.

48a

48a. Running figures in various parts of southern Africa sometimes have their legs stretched out. They give the impression of great fleetness.
48b. Women are depicted much less frequently than men. Various reasons have been advanced to explain this difference. Whatever the explanation, we must remember that Bushman rock art is not a simple portrayal of the real world. Even the depictions of animals do not reflect the true proportions of the various species in the environment. There is therefore no reason why we should expect men and women to be depicted in more or less equal proportions. If we recall that there are more male than female shamans in Bushman society (p. 32), we should not be surprised to find that men outnumber women in the spirit world depicted on the rocks. More men than women explore that world.

When women are depicted, they are sometimes dancing (18); more frequently (but not always), they are performing one of two activities: carrying digging sticks (53e) or clapping (16a). Whether seated or standing, they are usually wearing some kind of back or front apron. It is only in the Eland Bull Dance of the girls' puberty rituals (p. 119) that women remove their back aprons.

48b

49a. Some human figures are painted in great detail. They may have lines at the wrist and ankle, as well as just below the knee. These lines probably depict bead, skin or fibre bangles. Whereas some of these may have been merely decorative, others were particularly associated with the trance dance. Commenting on a copy of a rock painting depicting a dance, one of Bleek's /Xam informants said that the 'rings' were 'the //ken's rings'. //ken is one of the words the /Xam used to mean supernatural potency (p. 32). The man went on to say that the rings were made from //gwi:, an edible root, or from animal skin. Bleek was unable to identify the root, but the man described it as long and having a milky juice; it also had a fibrous outside from which the rings were made. The modern !Kung still wear rings of animal skin, but they are not associated specifically with the dance, although they are believed to have potency and to bring good fortune by enabling a man to run faster and shoot better.

49b. Occasionally, human figures have a fairly wide band at the waist. Because the genitals are sometimes shown, it seems unlikely that these bands depict articles of clothing. The constricted waists of many of these figures suggest that the bands depict the physical sensation described by an old !Kung shaman who told Megan Biesele that, when he entered trance, his 'sides were pressed by pieces of metal. Metal things fastened to my sides.'

49c. There are a number of ways in which the human head is depicted. The absence of facial features from most Bushman rock paintings has been taken to reflect a belief in magic, but there is no evidence for this. Most heads are simply a round blob; others are 'concave', or rather prognathous (with projecting jaws). A particularly distinctive type has the top and back of the head and the neck painted in a dark colour (usually red) and the face in white. When the more fugitive white paint fades, a 'hook' or question-mark shape is left.

49a

49b

49c

50. All the handprints in southern Africa are positive: that is, paint was applied to the hand which was then pressed against the rock face. Handprints are found principally in the western Cape and less frequently in the Waterberg. They are extremely rare, or entirely absent, throughout the southeastern mountains. It has been argued that their distribution suggests that they were made by Khoikhoi herders rather than by Bushmen, but there are reasons for disputing this claim. Some authors have argued that their size suggests a diminutive people and therefore Bushmen rather than Khoikhoi.

There are two kinds of handprint in southern Africa: plain and decorated. The plain ones were made by applying paint all over the hand. Decorated prints were made by applying paint to the hand and then scraping it off to form curved lines looping across the palm before pressing the hand against the rock face. These decorated prints may hold a clue to the meaning of handprints.

At one time it was thought that handprints signified ownership, a 'signature', or simply 'I was here'. But the large numbers that occur in some sites and other points argue against so simple an explanation. We turn to neuropsychology for some light on their origin and to Bushman beliefs for insight into their meaning. In the first place, the decorated prints recall the nested U-shaped entoptic phenomenon (26) that was, in some areas, construed as honeycombs (27a). If this is a valid observation, the inference is that potency was associated with the hands. This is very probable because Bushman shamans cured by the laying on of hands and drawing sickness out of a patient and into their own bodies. One of Wilhelm Bleek's /Xam men said that a shaman who had pleaded he had lost his ability to cure had said, 'Why do you ask this? Do you think my hands feel as they used to do? For my hands have become weak.'

He was suggesting that a particular feeling in the hands was associated with potency and curing. We know from other evidence that feelings experienced in trance are an important element in Bushman shamanism and rock art (22, 30, 31, 34, 49b).

It thus seems probable that making handprints in a rock shelter was, at least in some ways, akin to painting eland. Both practices fixed potency on the walls. Some shelters are crowded with eland paintings, others with handprints. Perhaps, as the old southern Bushwoman claimed about paintings of eland (p. 36), dancers could turn to the 'handmade' symbols of power when they wished to increase their potency.

50

People do evil and fight
When they have grown fat
After rain has fallen

> Wilhelm Bleek's informant
> Diä!kwain
> 1874

51

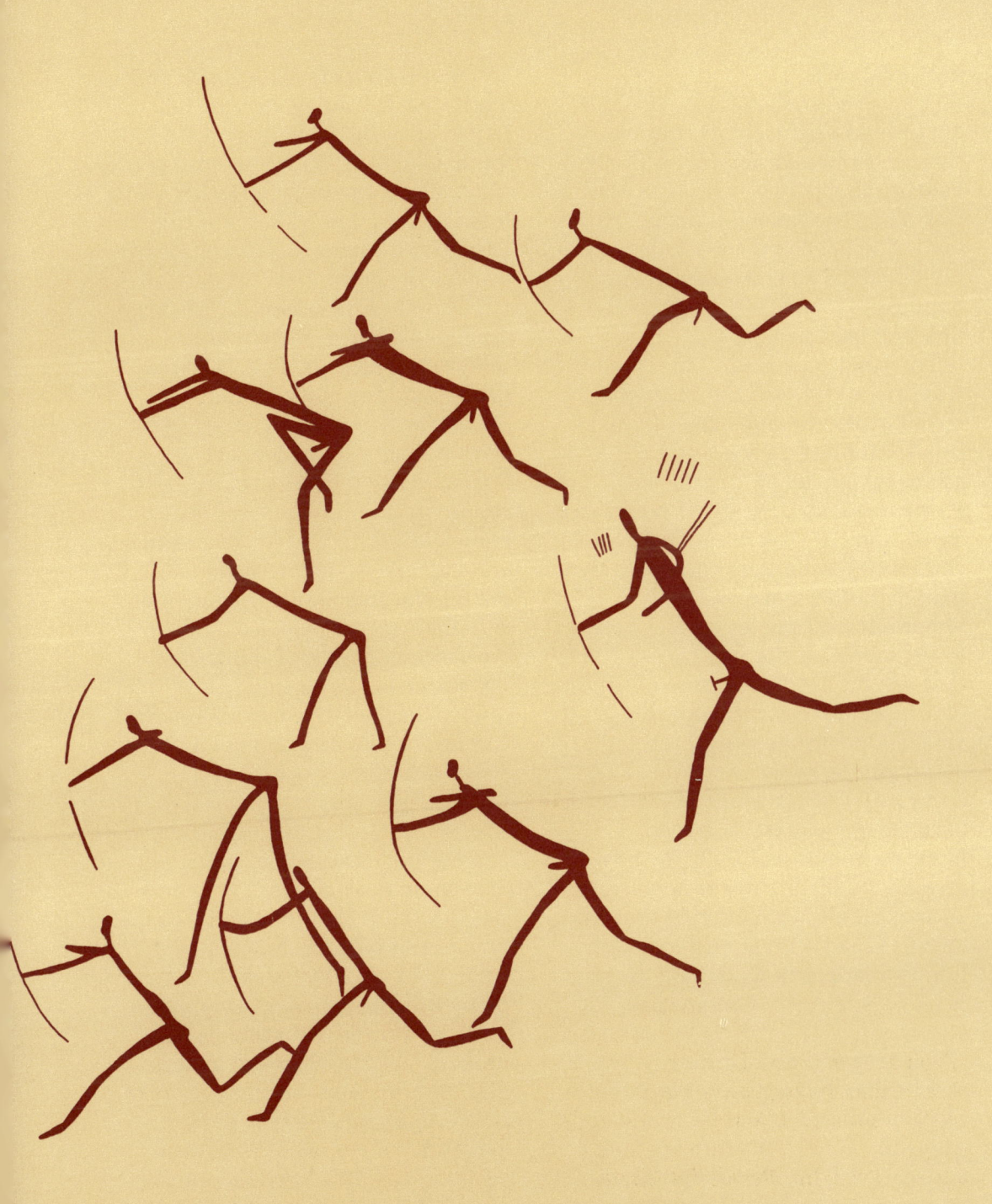

EQUIPMENT

52. In Bushman rock art, human figures carry a variety of equipment. One of the most interesting is the link-shaft or sectioned arrow. This kind of arrow comprises four parts which are distinguishable in many paintings (14, 46, 54): point, collar, link and shaft.

The point was traditionally made from stone or bone, but in more recent times the Bushmen obtained iron from black farmers (68-69) and white colonists (70, 71). In the Kalahari today, triangular points are made from fencing wire. Each point is distinctive: hunters recognise their own and others' arrows. This is important because an animal belongs to the owner of the fatal arrow, and that person has the responsibility for distributing the meat equitably amongst all the people in the camp. Another way of ensuring that everyone receives a fair share is the exchange of arrows. If a man is having a run of bad luck, he may give one of his arrows to a more successful hunter, knowing that any animal killed with it will belong to him and be his to distribute. In this way, no one goes hungry while others eat.

The second part of the arrow is a short collar that joins the point to a torpedo-shaped link of bone or wood. This link, in turn, fits into the fourth and last part, the reed shaft. When an arrow strikes an animal, the force of the impact drives the link into the collar and splits it. Collar, link and shaft then fall away, leaving the poisoned point embedded in the animal. With the long shaft out of the way, the arrow will not readily work loose as the animal flees; nor can the animal rub against a tree and easily remove the point.

The poison for which the Bushmen are famous is placed behind the point so as not to blunt it. The /Xam told Bleek that they made their arrow poison from snake venom and certain plants. The Kalahari Bushmen use the larvae of the beetle *Diamphidia simplex*. There is no known antidote, and the Bushmen are very careful indeed to avoid getting the poison into their eyes or onto their skin. The poison affects the nervous system of the animal, and the meat can be eaten quite safely, although the discoloured flesh around the wound is cut out and discarded.

The poison may take some days to take effect. During this time the hunters track the animal until they come upon it. Sometimes they find that the animal has died and that the hyenas and vultures have eaten it. If it is not dead, they dispatch it with a spear.

The Bushman bow is comparatively puny, and a hunter has to stalk up close to be sure of a fatal shot. The art seems to show bows of different kinds: well curved (52b), comparatively straight (52c), and triple curved. It is possible that the extremely elongated bows shown in some paintings are not 'realistic'.

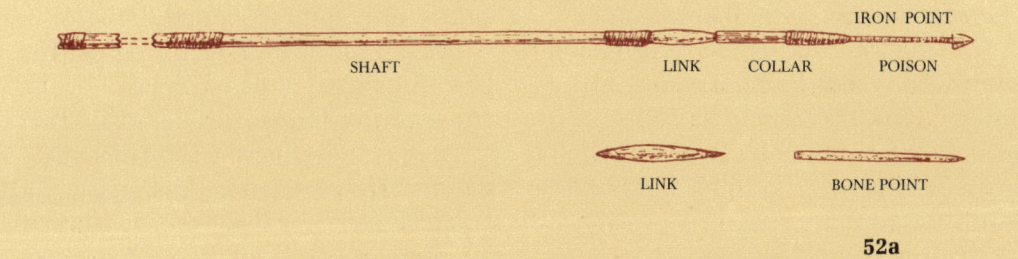

IRON POINT
SHAFT   LINK   COLLAR   POISON

LINK   BONE POINT

52a

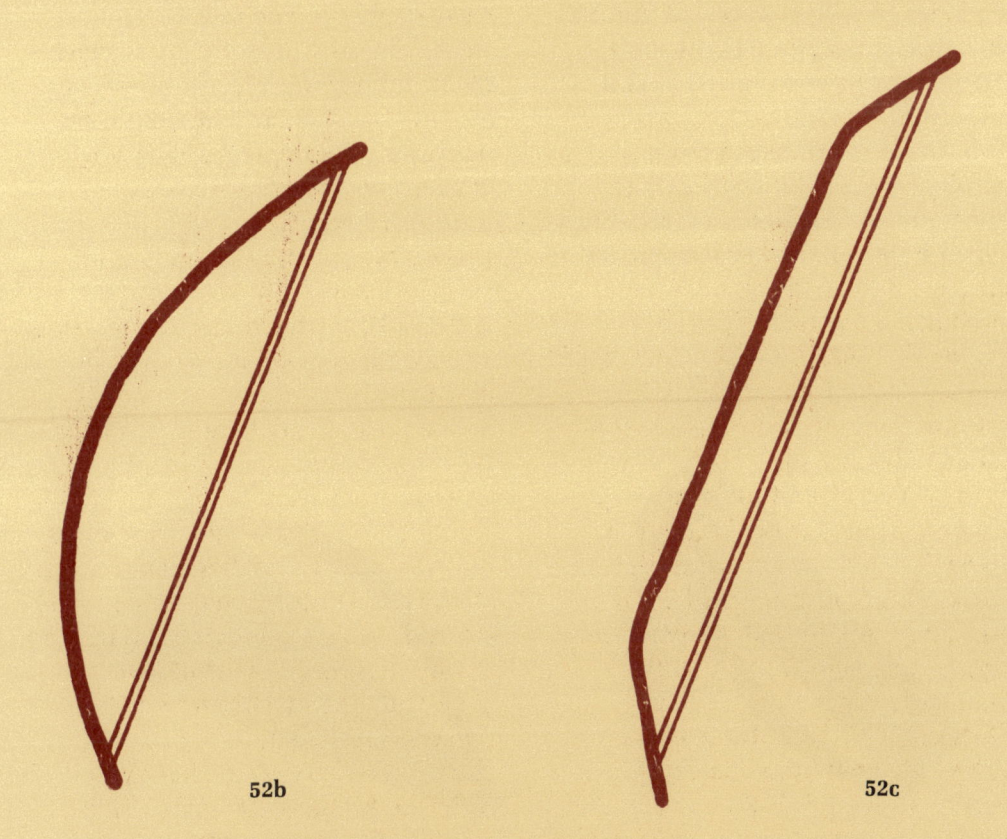

52b   **52c**

Men carry their arrows in a quiver, usually made of bark (**53a**). The quiver, bow and other pieces of equipment are carried in a skin hunting-bag (**53b**) which is wider at one end than the other and which has a thong running its length so that it can be slung over a shoulder. Some paintings depict tufted sticks (**53c**) protruding from these bags or separately. The southern Bushmen used sticks topped with feathers, which were stuck in the ground in long rows to deflect antelope into an ambush. Sometimes it is difficult to distinguish between tufted sticks and flywhisks (16d).

Another kind of bag is more rectangular and has a carry thong curved above the opening (**53d**). Both men and women use these bags.

Modern examples are often decorated with ostrich eggshell beads, and painted examples sometimes have white dots. In other paintings these dots represent supernatural potency (30c, 34a).

The most distinctive item of women's equipment is the digging stick. Sometimes these were weighted with bored stones (**53e**). A hole was laboriously bored through these stones, and they were fixed onto the stick with wooden wedges. They made digging in hard ground easier. Bored stones are not used in the Kalahari, where suitable stones are rare and the sand is comparatively soft. Examples greatly varying in size have been found all over southern Africa.

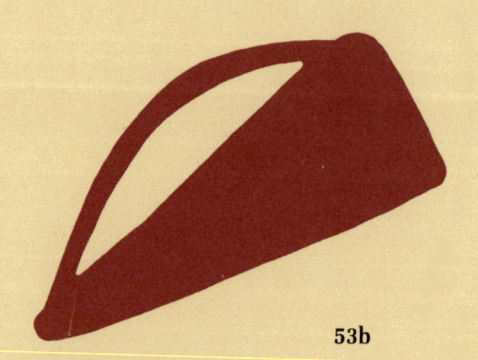

53b

53c

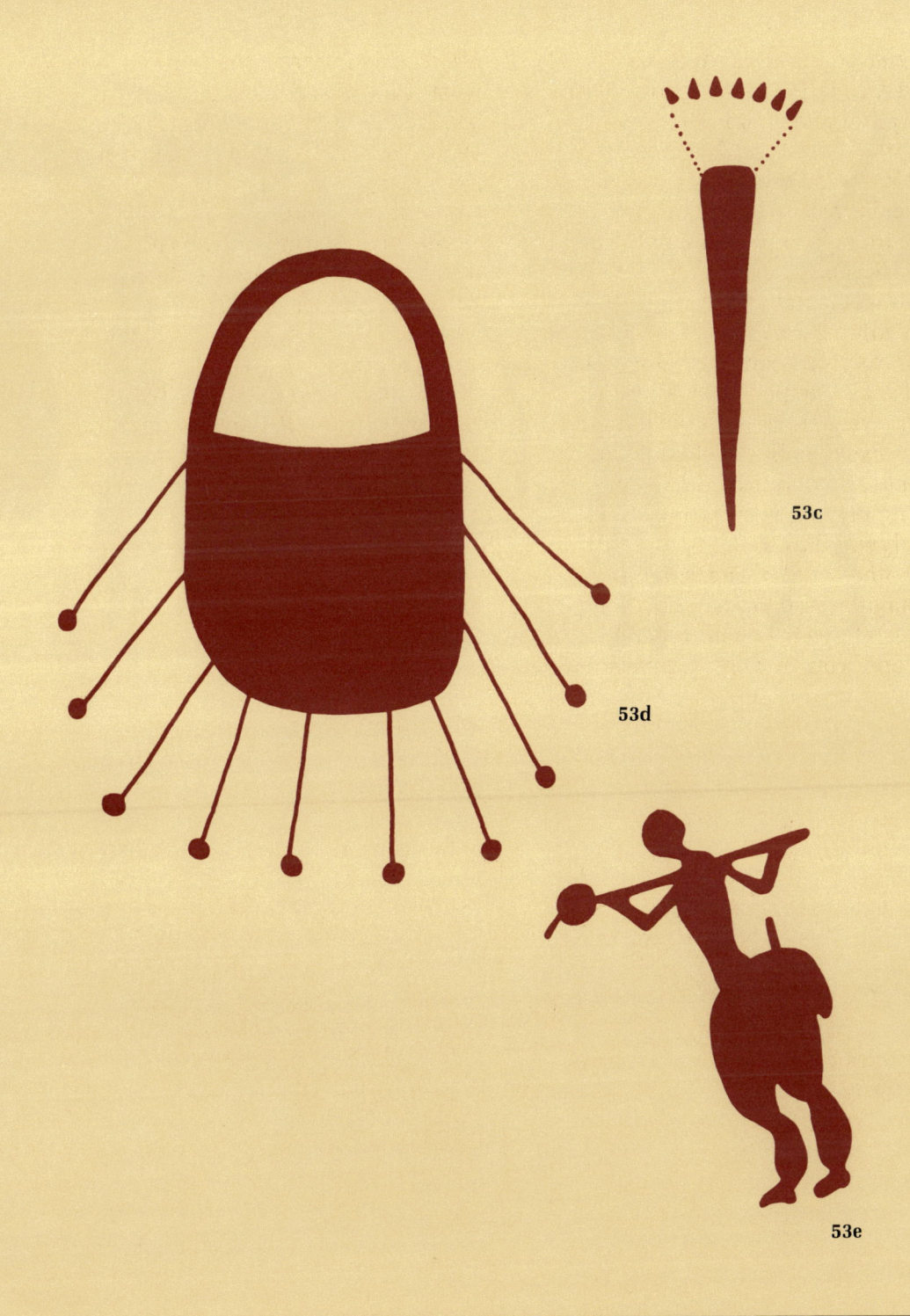

53d

53e

Bows, arrows, bags and digging sticks may seem to be perfectly ordinary items of equipment, but there is more to them than meets the eye.

54. A painting in the Natal Drakensberg exemplifies this point very well. In the centre there are numerous seated figures, one of whom is in the hand-to-nose posture (19a). To the right, a man stands in the arms-back posture (17). These two figures show that the group is, in some way, connected with trance. Above the figures there is a line of bags: there are four hunting bags and three carrying bags. At the right there are three digging sticks with bored stones. Whereas it could be argued that the people have simply laid aside their equipment while they dance and clap, the records of Bushman beliefs suggest that bags and digging sticks had special significance beyond everyday use.

In the myth 'A visit to the Lion's house', the Mantis (p. 13) frightens the Little Lion by hiding in a bag and 'winking' at the child. When the Lioness approaches, the Mantis 'gets feathers', flies up into the sky and then dives into a waterhole. We know that flying and diving into waterholes are metaphors for trance experience (22, 23). Moreover, the word Lloyd translated as 'winking' means to flutter the eyes as in dying – a further reference to trance (20). It therefore seems very likely that the bag is another member of this set of

54

trance metaphors. How the bag came to have this association may be explained by the Bushman belief that an artefact is not to be distinguished from the substance of which it is made. Getting into a skin bag was therefore equivalent to getting into an animal – that is, taking on its potency. Bags painted next to a dance, or indeed by themselves, thus probably signify trance experience rather than merely discarded equipment.

Digging sticks had similar associations. When a /Xam woman wished to address shamans of the game, possibly including dead shamans, she beat upon the ground with a bored stone from her digging stick. Speaking of this practice, an informant's mother said, 'I will just beat the ground to see what is affecting my husband's going. His hunting is not fortunate.' Another woman stuck her digging stick upright in the ground when she asked a chameleon if it would rain. It seems, then, that digging sticks were involved with contacting the supernatural world, the principal purpose of the trance dance.

The whole painted group is thus a coherent symbolic whole: all its parts complement one another and refer, in various ways, to the shamans' work and experience. Once again, an understanding of Bushman belief throws new light on the art.

117

ANIMALS

For the Bushmen, animals mean much more than just food. It is therefore essential that we understand Bushman beliefs about and attitudes towards the animals they painted and engraved.

Megan Biesele described how the !Kung recite lists of animals in a highly stylised, rhapsodic fashion:

The first syllable goes way down in tone. The second, the pluralisation, goes up and then comes down again, trailing off from near-singing into silence. N!ghwasi,... /hausi,... n!si,... dwasi... (Kudus,... buffaloes,... elands,... giraffes,...).

The !Kung are so enthralled by these recitations that, as Biesele saw, 'almost, the eyes glaze over'. A century and more ago, and hundreds of kilometres to the south, Wilhelm Bleek recorded the same practice. He was so impressed by the way the /Xam called out the names that he used the word 'incantation'.

Biesele realised that these performances were a celebration of the power of animals:

The impression of multitudinous animal richness in these listings was very strong. With access to some of that power, one felt, a person could do anything.

There are several areas of life in which Bushmen feel they cannot cope by themselves: they must reach out for supernatural power. Curing the sick, going on out-of-body journeys, and controlling the movements of antelope herds – all tasks of the shamans – demand this extra power. Animals, because they are visibly powerful and at hand, are seen as a source of the desired power. In Biesele's words, animals are 'metaphors with the strength to bridge worlds'. According to one !Kung shaman, god, the source of all potency, is surrounded by animals: 'Elands are there. Giraffes are there. Gemsboks are there. Kudus are there ... They are god's possessions.'

Eland

55-59. Chief amongst all these animals is the eland. It is, of course, the largest of southern African antelope and is much desired as a source of meat and fat. But the Bushmen go further and say that all other animals are like servants to the eland. As a major symbol in Bushman thought, the eland appears in four important rituals: boys' first-kill, girls' puberty, marriage, and the trance dance. To obtain some understanding of what the eland meant to the Bushmen, we shall look in turn at the part it played in each of these rituals.

A !Kung boy becomes an adult when he kills his first large antelope, ideally an eland. When the wounded eland has been tracked down, the adult men remove its skin and the boy sits on it. They then scarify him with fat from a broth made from the eland's throat and collar bone, both of which are believed to have much potency. The cuts are said to 'create a new hunter'. Then, while the seated boy holds his bow pointing out in front of him, an old man takes the right foreleg of the eland, or the left if it is female, and makes a circle of hoofprints around the skin on which the boy is sitting. As this is being done, the eland hoof emits the characteristic clicking sound which the animal makes as it walks. The circle of hoofprints is made so that, when the boy hunts eland in future, he will easily find their spoor. Throughout the ritual, the boy keeps his eyes downcast: 'That is how elands will behave when he hunts them in future.' Then the boy drops the bow, plucking the string with his thumb as he does so; this is how the eland will fall when he goes to hunt.

In the girls' puberty rituals, a young girl is, at her first menstruation, isolated in a hut. Then, after most of the men have left the camp, the women perform the Eland Bull Dance. As they dance around the hut, they imitate the mating behaviour of eland cows. An old man plays the part of the eland bull and either wears horns or holds up two blackened sticks to represent horns. At the climax of the dance, so the !Kung say, an eland approaches and frightens the people, but a shaman reassures them that it is 'a good thing come from god'.

Throughout the dance there is a close association between the eland and the girl in the hut: 'The eland is a good thing and has much fat. And the girl is also a good thing and she is all fat. Therefore they are called the same thing.'

Why do they perform the Eland Bull Dance? An old !Kung woman explained:

They do the Eland Bull Dance so that she will be well; she will be beautiful; that she won't be thin; so that if there is hunger, she won't be very hungry and she won't be terribly thirsty, and she will be peaceful. That all will go well with the land and that rain will fall.

Inside the hut, the girl weeps, overcome by the wonder of it all.

As part of the marriage rituals, a young !Kung man hunts an eland and gives the fat of the eland's heart to the girl's mother. At a later stage the bride is annointed with eland fat.

In the trance dance, the eland is considered the most potent of all animals, and shamans aspire to possess eland potency. When they are dancing eland potency, eland are supposed to be attracted to the place, and the shamans see them, spirit elands, standing in the darkness beyond the camp fire. They direct one another's attention to these eland, so pooling their apprehension of the spirit world. The association between the eland and the trance dance is so close that the !Kung use the word *tcheni*, dance, as a respect word for eland.

All these associations – first-kill, girls' puberty, marriage, trance – add up to constitute the eland's exceptional potency. No wonder that the southern Bushmen believed the eland to be /Kaggen's (the Mantis's) favourite animal. One of Wilhelm Bleek's informants said that the Mantis sits between the eland's horns. The eland was also the Mantis's first creation and he loved it dearly: 'The Mantis does not love us, if we kill an eland.' Sometimes he went to a wounded eland and made it recover from the poison. When the Meerkats killed the first Eland, the Mantis was greatly distressed: 'He called the Eland, it did not come. Then he wept; tears fell from his eyes, because he did not see the Eland.'

It is these and other aspects of Bushman beliefs about eland that explain why it is the most frequently depicted animal in many regions of southern Africa. It is also the animal on which the artists lavished most care. More paintings of eland are done in the complex and time-consuming polychrome technique than of any other animal. In these paintings the upper part of the animal is painted in red, while the neck and belly are done in white. The hoofs, back line and other details are painted in black. Furthermore, the artists seem to have gone out of their way to paint the

55

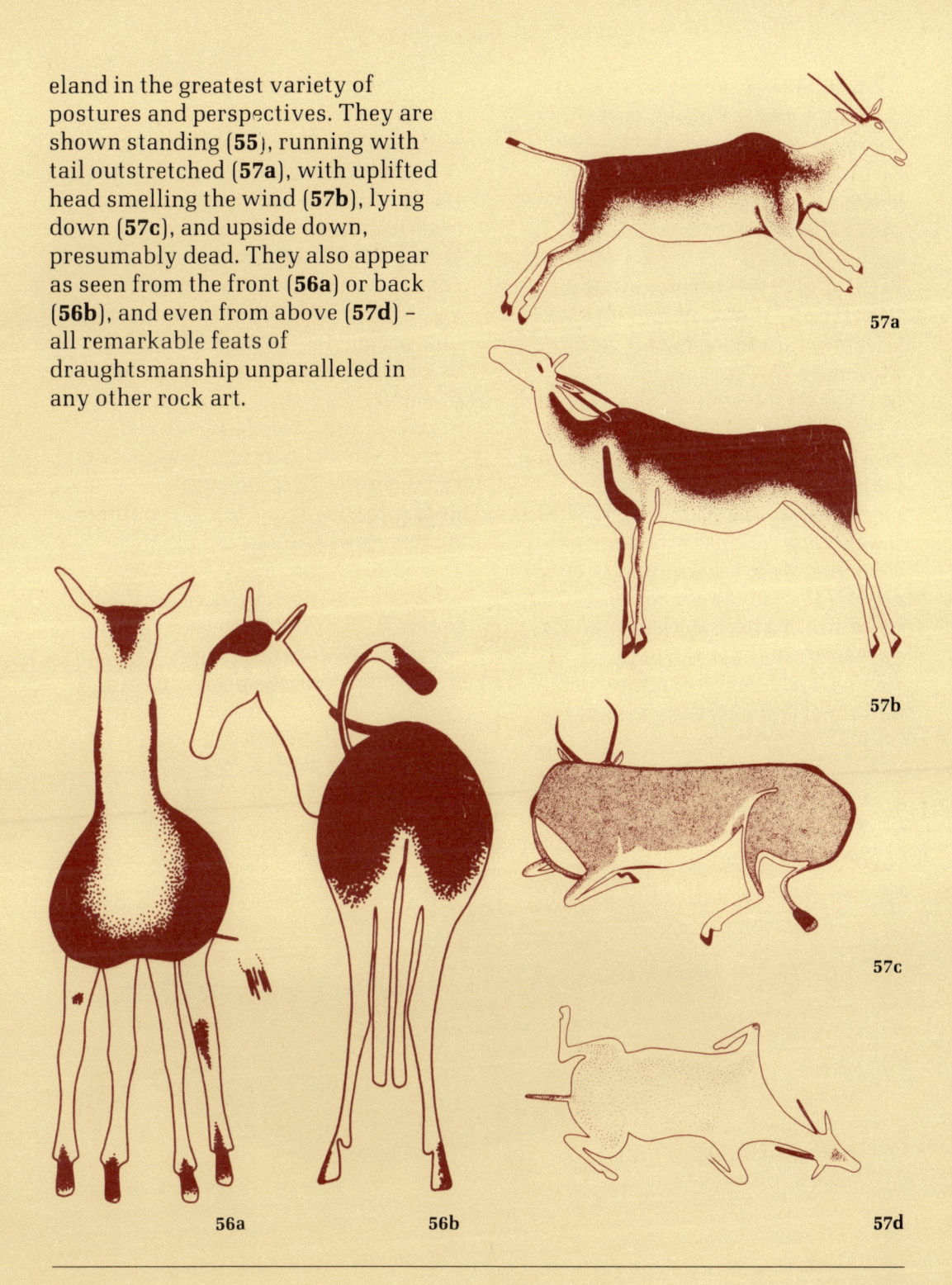

eland in the greatest variety of postures and perspectives. They are shown standing (**55**), running with tail outstretched (**57a**), with uplifted head smelling the wind (**57b**), lying down (**57c**), and upside down, presumably dead. They also appear as seen from the front (**56a**) or back (**56b**), and even from above (**57d**) – all remarkable feats of draughtsmanship unparalleled in any other rock art.

57a

57b

56a **56b**

57c

57d

121

The paintings are so accurately done that modern !Kung men shown copies of rock paintings were able to identify the age, sex and type of eland. One with a sagging back (**58a**) they called *chai*, 'father of little elands'. Perhaps they were referring to the role the eland plays in the puberty and marriage rituals.

Some of these ideas may be expressed in a unique rock engraving that shows an eland with a male and a female belly line, a large male dewlap and a smaller female dewlap (**58b**). This depiction may be explained by the Bushman belief that the eland is in some way bisexual. They point out that in most antelope species the female has more fat than the male, but with the eland this is uniquely reversed: the male has more fat than the female. In other paintings and engravings, eland are depicted with vastly exaggerated dewlaps that emphasise the male eland's quantity of fat (**58c**).

It should now be clear that, when the Bushmen looked at paintings and engravings of eland, their response was far richer and more complex than ours. For them, the animal signified goodness and potency, and was associated with god himself. Rock shelters with extensive panels of eland, piled up in all sorts of postures and perspectives, must have had a very dramatic impact on the Bushmen. It is easy to understand why, as the old southern Bushwoman pointed out (p. 36), shamans turned to these panels when they wished to increase their potency. In Biesele's elegant phrase, the paintings of eland were metaphors with the power to bridge worlds.

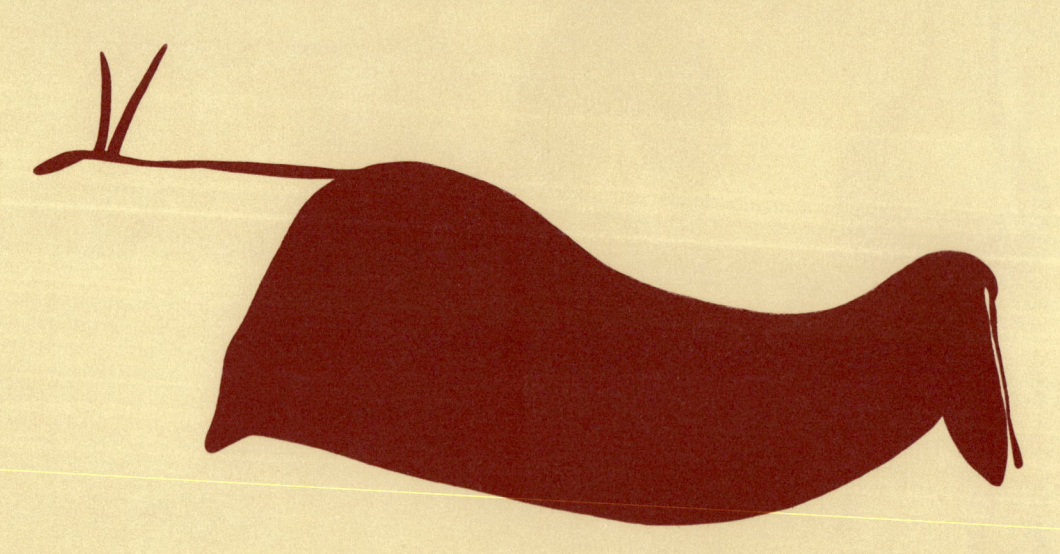

58a

58b

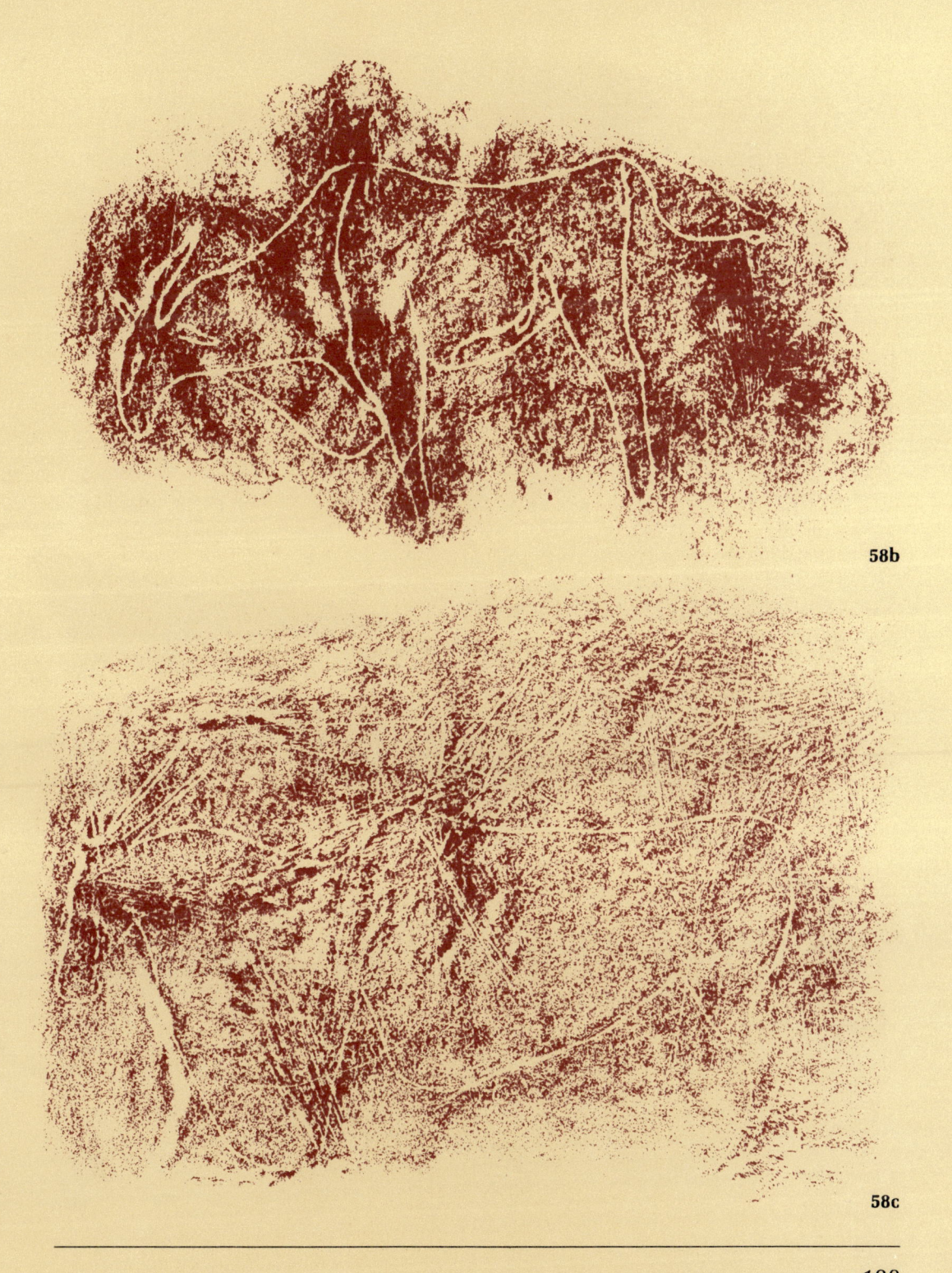

58c

59

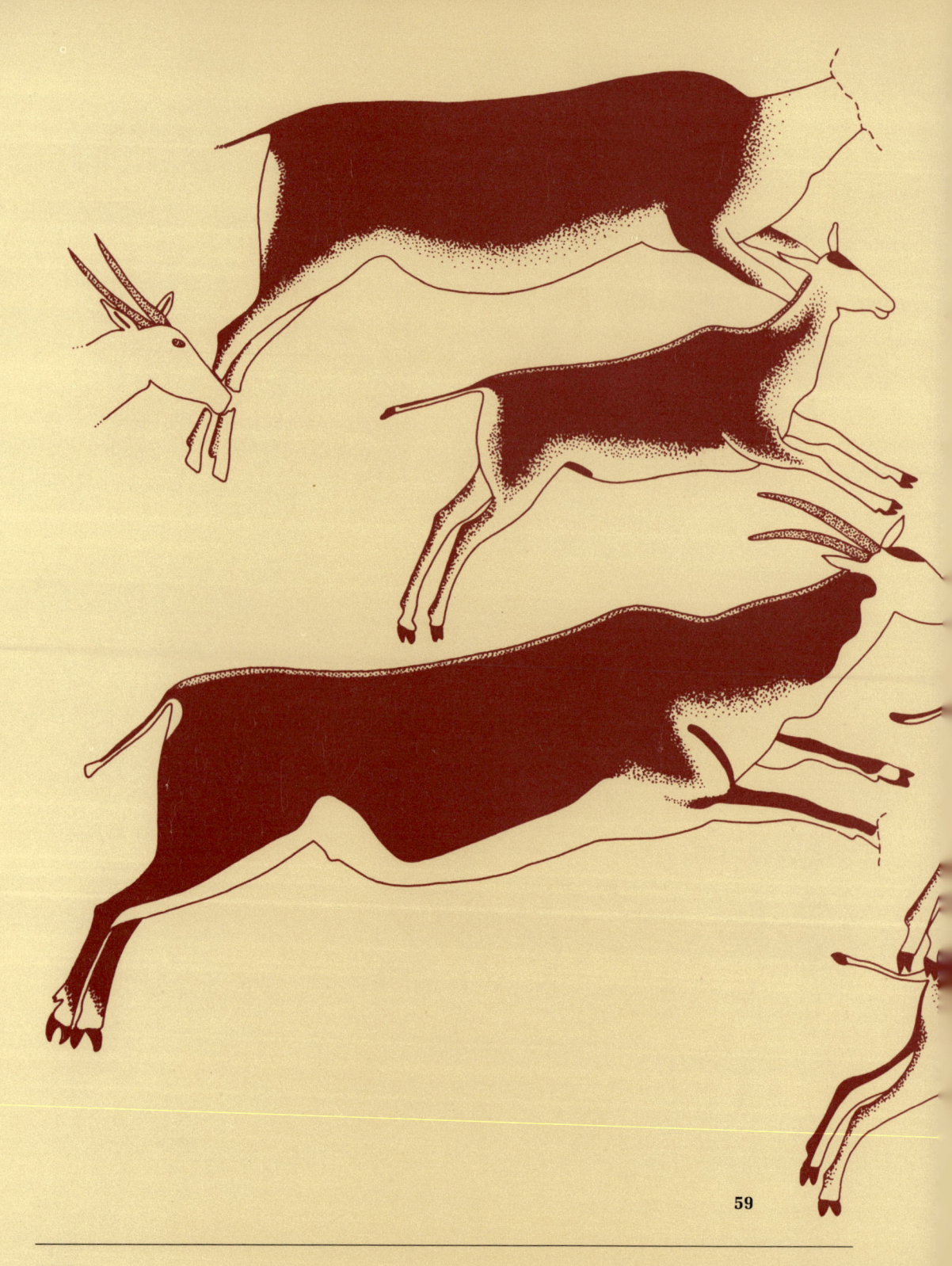

Where is /Kaggen?

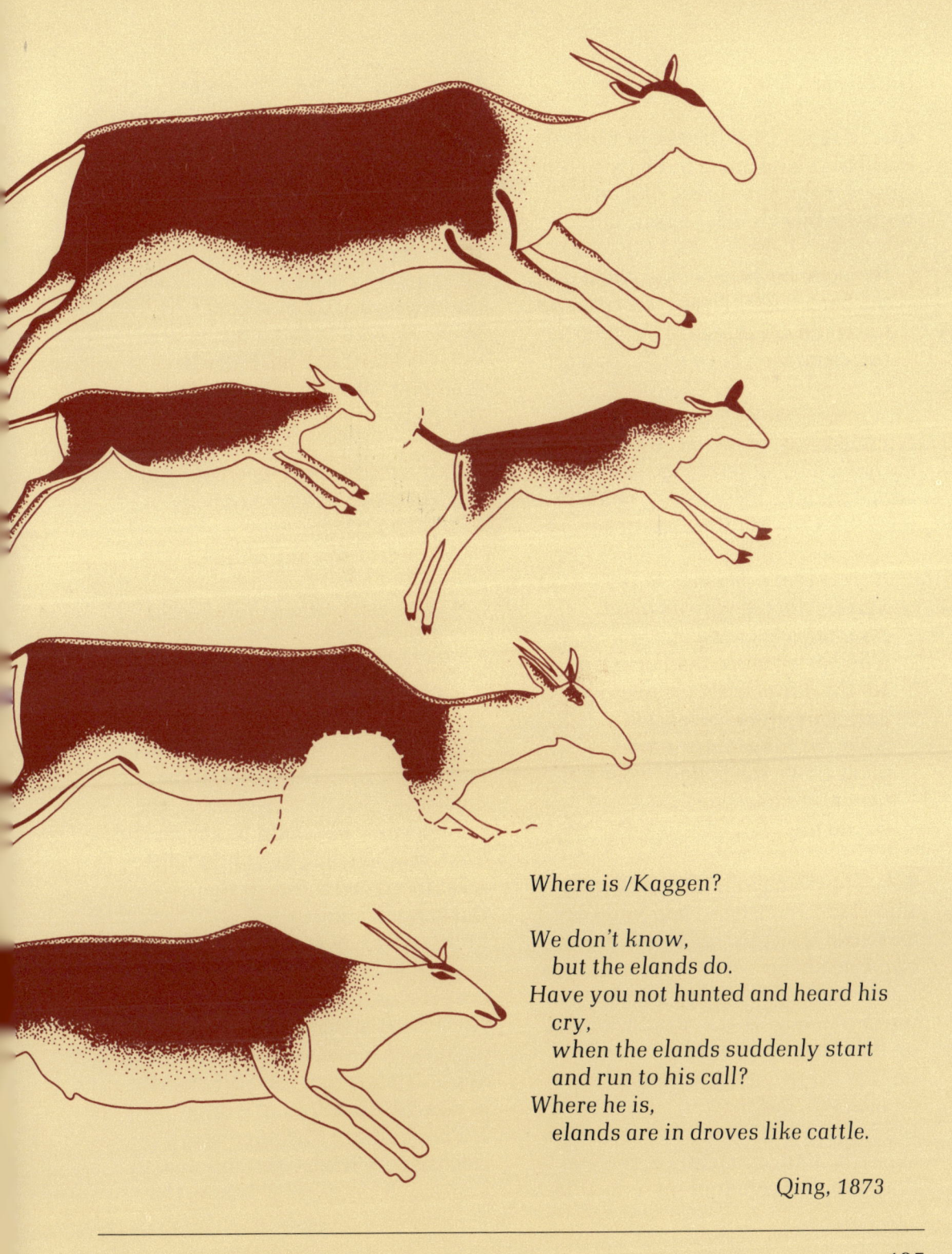

We don't know,
　but the elands do.
Have you not hunted and heard his
　cry,
　　when the elands suddenly start
　and run to his call?
Where he is,
　elands are in droves like cattle.

　　　　　　　　　　Qing, 1873

Hartebeest, kudu and wildebeest

60a. /Kaggen (the Mantis, p. 13) loved the eland most, but he also cared for the hartebeest. One of Wilhelm Bleek's informants said,

> He made his heart of the eland and the hartebeest. The hartebeest and the eland are things of the Mantis; therefore they have magic power.

The 'magic power' to which he was referring was, of course, the potency harnessed by shamans (p. 32). He added that the hartebeest's head resembles the Mantis's head:

> It feels that it belongs to the Mantis: that is why its head resembles his head. A woman who has a young child does not eat the hartebeest, nor does she spring over the hartebeest's head, for the Mantis would press down the hollow place on her child's head, and the child would die.

60b. The !Kung told Megan Biesele that eland, hartebeest and kudu are 'red meat' animals and are therefore appropriate for use in rituals such as the boys' first-kill. They also have much potency. 'Black meat' animals, on the other hand, are less potent, but the !Kung, being a pragmatic people, will use them in rituals if no red-meat animals are available. This classification of animals according to the supposed colour of their meat is interesting because the artists depicted far more red- than black-meat animals.

60c. The wildebeest (gnu), a black-meat animal, is infrequently depicted compared with other large antelope. Its rarity has given rise to some speculation because the Bushmen definitely ate it. Arbousset and Daumas, who in the 1830s visited what is now Lesotho, recorded a Bushman 'prayer' addressed to /Kaggen:

> /Kaggen, lead me to a male gnu.
> I like much to have my belly filled;
> My oldest son, my oldest daughter,
> Like much to have their bellies filled.
> /Kaggen, bring a male gnu under my darts.

/Kaggen answered through the head movements of a bagworm. If it moved its head in a semicircle, the hunter knew he would be successful. That very evening he would hold meat in his teeth and, in the Bushman fashion, cut it with his knife, 'with thy arm bent, and describing also a semicircle'. If this prayer and the fact that Bushmen ate wildebeest are contrasted with the paucity of wildebeest depictions, the implication is that the art has little to do with hunting and eating.

The southern Bushmen also consider the wildebeest inimical to hunting. A myth records how the

Wildebeest blunted the Longnosed Mouse's arrows. Then, when the Longnosed Mice tried to ambush the Quaggas, the Wildebeest trampled on their screen of bushes. This is what the Bushmen call 'angry' behaviour. Biesele heard a !Kung tale in which a man is said to be 'angry'. He is in fact a wildebeest.

All these Bushman beliefs are linked and help to explain why they painted and engraved some animals frequently and others hardly at all.

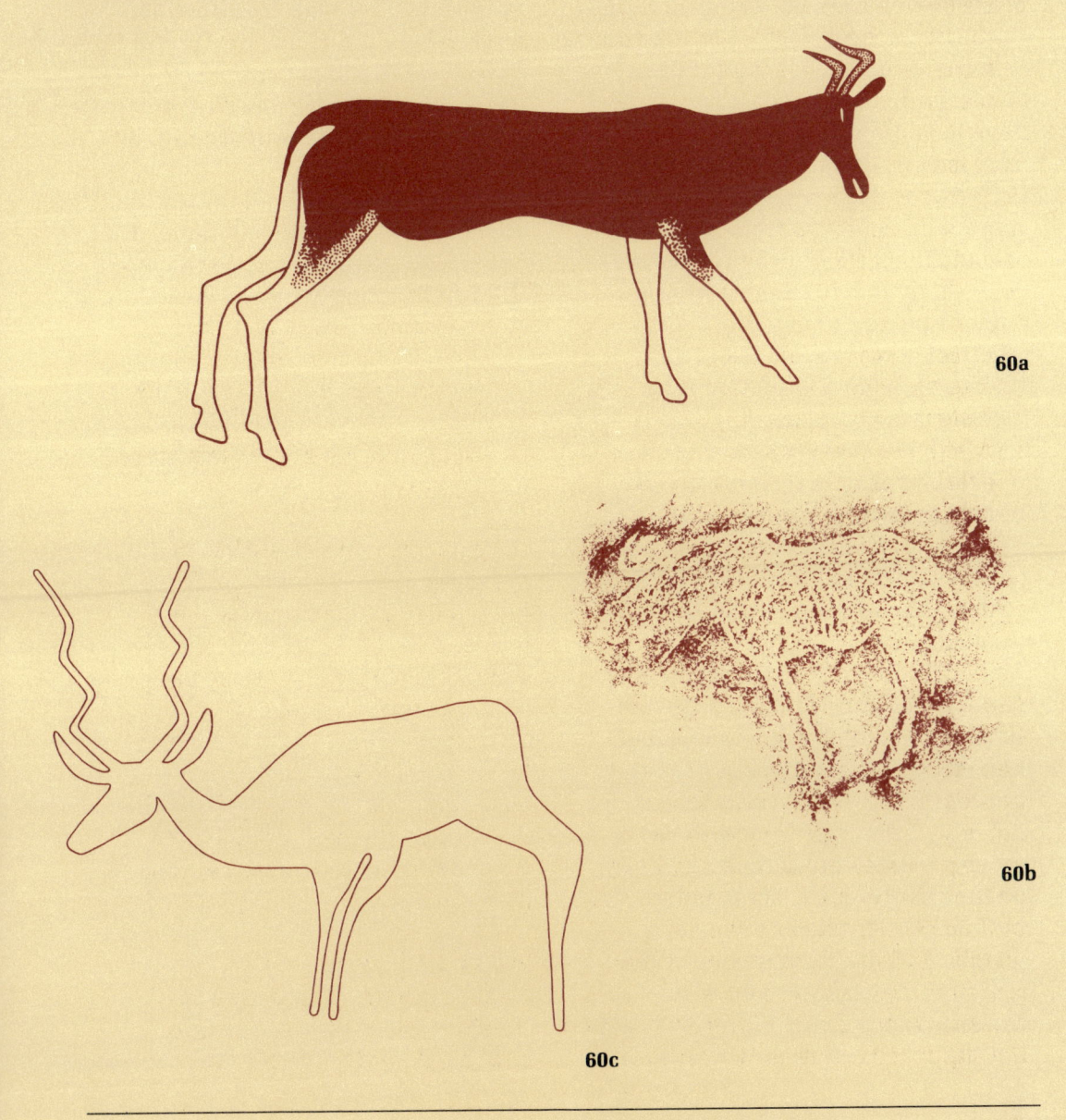

60a

60b

60c

127

Small antelope

61. It is often impossible to distinguish the exact species of small antelope depicted in Bushman rock art. Horns, a good means of identification, are frequently not preserved or were not depicted in the first place.

In the southeastern mountains, after eland, the next most frequently depicted antelope is rhebuck. This term is used loosely to cover grey rhebuck, or vaalribbok (*Perlea capreolus*), and mountain reedbuck, or rooiribbok (*Redunca fulvorufula*). Grey rhebuck have a somewhat bulbous nose, and mountain reedbuck have longer, swept-back horns. While the distinctive grey rhebuck nose is sometimes clearly depicted, the absence of horns often makes confident identification of mountain reedbuck impossible. Frequently, it is safer to use only the general word 'rhebuck'.

Rhebuck are, interestingly, associated with eland in the way they are painted and also in a myth Orpen heard from Qing in 1873. In the first place, Pat Vinnicombe has pointed out that rhebuck are frequently painted in two colours, red and white, as are eland, even though rhebuck are actually predominantly grey. Then, in Qing's myth, a 'chief' named Qwanciqutshaa killed a 'red rhebuck'. When he was skinning it, he saw 'his elands running about'. Qing also said that the 'men with rhebok heads ... tame eland and snakes'. This puzzling remark is actually a valuable clue to the meaning of paintings of rhebuck. We know that the men with rhebuck heads are shamans (30). We also know that the creature Qing said they catch is a rain-animal (42-45). He added that he could tell they had been 'spoilt by the dance' (p. 29) because their noses bleed (15). They are therefore specifically shamans of the rain in trance.

With this background understanding, we can see that 'tame' is a poor English translation of the word /ki, which actually means the

61a

shamans' ability to possess or to control animals. The shamans with rhebuck heads thus controlled eland and harnessed their power to enter trance and to perform their various tasks, including rain-making. Although we still do not fully understand these beliefs, Qing's remarks show conclusively that rhebuck were in some way associated with shamans.

In other regions where rhebuck are absent, springbok are sometimes depicted. They seem to have had associations similar to those of rhebuck. Bleek's /Xam people said that springbok possess invisible magic arrows (14). If people did not treat springbok bones respectfully or if they allowed children to play on a springbok skin, these supernatural arrows would kill them. In other words, springbok were, for them, like shamans – as were rhebuck for Qing's people. That is one of the reasons why the /Xam made caps (46) and dancing rattles (17) from springbok ears.

In a charming statement, one of Bleek's informants took the association between the Bushmen and springbok even further:

We who are Bushmen were once springbok, and the Mantis shot us, and we really cried like a little child. Then the Mantis said we should become a person, become people because we really cried.

61b

Snakes

62. Rock paintings of snakes are not uncommon. Often it is impossible to detect the head because the snake is entering or leaving a crack or step in the rock face, or even a white run left by seeping water. When the head is visible, it often has large 'tusks' (29), ears or a complete buck head (22); frequently it bleeds from the nose (15, 22). Sometimes a snake is painted so that it disappears behind a natural feature of the rock face and reappears on the other side. The dot and stripe patterns on these serpents seldom suggest a particular species. In fact, close inspection reveals that most of the painted snakes are not real snakes at all.

Bushman beliefs about snakes throw light on these puzzling features. When /Kaggen wanted to frighten a hunter who had shot one of his eland, he turned himself into a puff-adder. This transformation begins to make sense if we recall that /Kaggen was a shaman and could therefore change himself into various creatures by entering trance. The idea is developed in one of the myths Orpen recorded. Qwanciqutshaa, who is evidently also a shaman, turned himself into a snake and later 'glided out of the snake's skin' to collect 'charm food'. This food was 'canna', the hallucinogenic plant known in southern Africa as dagga and elsewhere as Indian hemp or marijuana. The Orpen myths tell about a number of transformations associated with canna.

The relationship between snakes and trance was further explained by Qing when he told Orpen that shamans 'whose charms are weak'

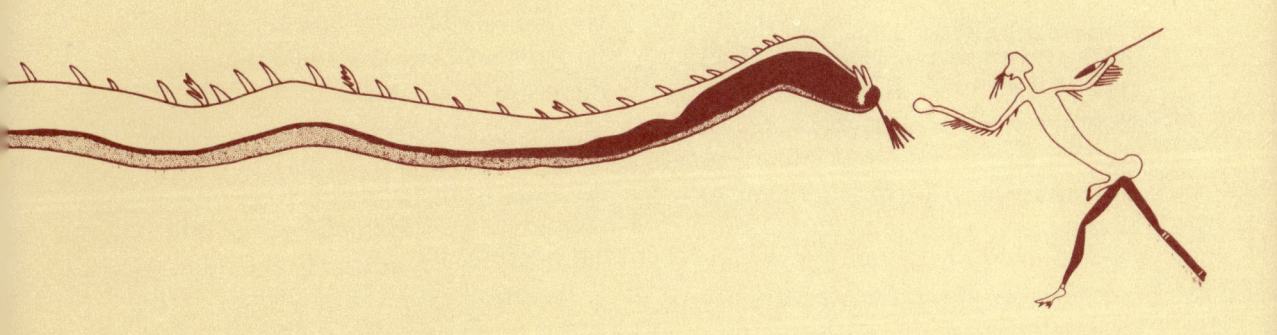

62

are given 'charm medicine' in which there is burnt snake powder. The snake powder helped them to control their level of trance.

One of the most illuminating pieces of information about snakes, and one that brings together the concepts we have already noted, comes from the //Xegwi Bushmen. E.F. Potgieter studied them in the eastern Transvaal, but they came originally from the southeastern mountains and spoke a dialect close to that of the /Xam. Their supreme being was /a'an, a variant of /Kaggen.

They told Potgieter that a //Xegwi man wishing to become a shaman had to plunge into a deep pool and come out with a snake 'as big as a python'. If it did not struggle as he ran to his hut with it, he was destined to be a shaman. Then he killed the snake and performed a public dance with the neck of the skin tied to his forehead and the rest trailing behind him.

Because this account is so rich in symbolism, it is not clear how much of it was actually performed. Whatever the case, there is a clear association between going underwater (22), snakes and shamans. This association was dramatised when the novice put on the snake skin and so virtually became a snake.

All these beliefs suggest very strongly that many of the painted serpents, especially those that bleed from the nose, *are* shamans in snake form – like /Kaggen and Qwanciqutshaa. Like snakes, shamans go underground and then surface again when on out-of-body travel, and this probably explains why painted snakes often seem to slither in and out of the rock face.

131

Felines

As may be expected of a people who lived in the open veld, Bushman lore is full of tales about lions. Some of these are personal anecdotes, others are clearly myths, and still others occupy a strange no man's land between reality and fantasy.

Lions in general were believed to have some of the shamans' accomplishments: they knew things that ordinary people could not possibly know, they could become invisible, and they could cause things to happen by supernatural means. They could also transform themselves into hartebeest and then, when the hunters appeared, revert to their feline form.

Not surprisingly, Bushmen believe shamans can turn themselves into lions. A !Kõ man told Heinz-Joachim Heinz that he could 'mix with' a pride of lions when he was in that form. The !Kung told Richard Katz that shamans were 'lions of god' and added that 'they were real lions, different from normal lions, but no less real'. Indeed, the !Kung go so far as to use the word for 'pawed creature' (*jum*) to mean 'to go on out-of-body travel in the form of a lion'. They told Ed Wilmsen that some shamans obtain lion-power by eating a lion's gall, which is believed to be the seat of its potency. So powerful is a man in the form of a lion that the /Xam believed that a lion that did not die when it had been shot was actually a shaman.

The !Kung also told Katz that, when malevolent shamans come marauding in feline form, the

shamans in the camp enter trance and chase them off. These threatening shaman-lions are invisible to ordinary people; only other shamans can see them: 'Then someone would shoot an arrow or throw a spear into these [shamans] who were prowling around as lions.'
63. Such a clash is depicted in a painting which shows men not merely running away from but shooting at two lions. The lions have the curious tusks which also occur on paintings of shamans, therianthropes (30, 31) and serpents (62). The painting also has scattered through it numerous flecks, similar to those found in some trance dance scenes (17, 25) and rain-making scenes. The painting therefore probably depicts a hallucinatory combat between benevolent shamans and attacking shaman-lions.

In many paintings it is less easy to distinguish the species of feline. Some have spots, but most have the long, curved tail characteristic of various species of feline.

The thinness of the dividing line between hallucination and reality inherent in many Bushman beliefs is illustrated by a /Xam tale. A man went on out-of-body travel in the form of a lion and killed a farmer's ox. The farmer discovered the dead ox, raised a commando and wounded the man. When the farmers pursued him, he had managed, in his wounded condition, to 'drive the people away', and they had become afraid. He struggled back to camp and told the informant's father that he should not forget what he had taught him about trance. Sadly, he died of his wounds.

63

Jackal and baboon

64a. The jackal, a pawed creature like the lion (63), was another animal into which a shaman could transform himself. A /Xam man said that 'a jackal who is a sorcerer' follows people who have been visiting him because he wants to see that they return home safely. At night, while they are encamped on the way home, he barks, and they know that 'he is asking us whether we are still as well as we were when we left him'. They shout out to him, 'There is nothing the matter with me, for I am still feeling as I did when I left you.' When they eventually reach home, they see him in his jackal persona, 'sitting opposite the hut'. Then, 'as soon as he sees that we are really among our people, he returns to his home'. A painting in the Orange Free State seems to illustrate just such a circumstance. It depicts two jackals with their characteristically bushy tails, but, remarkably, one of them carries a bag (53d).

64b. Baboons are painted and engraved more frequently than jackals, and they also feature more frequently in Bushman myth and folklore. Not surprisingly, it is the baboon's closeness to human beings that is prominent in Bushman beliefs about them. Samuel Dornan found that the Kalahari Bushmen considered baboons, springbok (61) and snakes (62) to be people in another state of existence, and Dorothea Bleek found that the Naron did not eat baboons because they are so like people.

The /Xam believed that, like the lion, the baboon had powers similar to those of shamans. It was supposed to derive those powers from a small stick of a plant called *sho:/õä*, which it kept in its left cheek. Unfortunately, *sho:/õä* has not been

64a

identified; it is simply described as a plant with a red top and long roots. It was used as a charm and may have been hallucinogenic. In any event, it enabled a baboon to know things beyond ordinary ken, to tell when danger was approaching, and to protect itself from illness. When a /Xam shaman killed a baboon, he removed the *sho:/õä* from its cheek and kept it. Baboons were also able to shoot arrows back at a man, as the Meerkats did when, having killed the first Eland and having appropriated its potency, they were attacked by the enraged /Kaggen.

A man who killed a baboon was required to take certain precautions. He had to cut fine lines around the points of his bow. If he failed to do this, 'the baboon's curse' would be in the bow.

The baboons also had the ≠*gebbi-gu* before people did. This Bushman word is difficult to understand, but it seems to mean songs sung at a dance. When, according to a /Xam myth, the Lion and the Ostrich fought, they lost the songs and people acquired them. Yet, it seems, the baboons retained the songs and still sing them.

Some depictions of baboons show a whole troop with males, females and babies clearly depicted. There are also therianthropic baboons (31b) which express the closeness of baboons to people and, more important, the association between baboons and shamans.

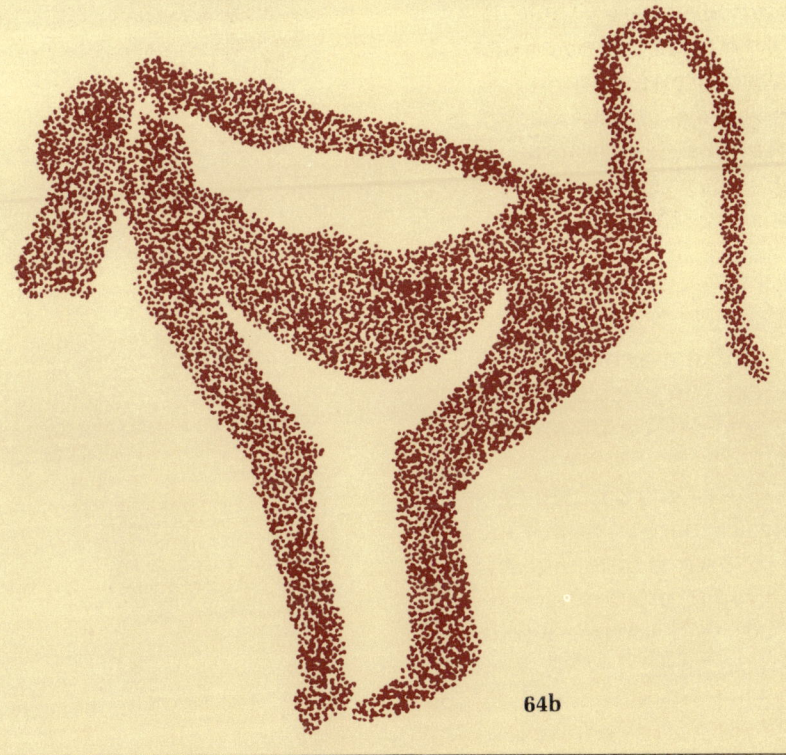

64b

Birds

Birds are infrequently depicted in Bushman rock art. Sometimes the species can be identified, but often this is not possible.

65a. In the Cape, the Orange Free State, the Transvaal and Namibia, and somewhat less frequently in the Natal Drakensberg, there are some fine paintings or engravings of ostriches. Lorna Marshall has pointed out that, for the !Kung, ostrich eggs have supernatural potency. Bushwomen make beads by boring through fragments of ostrich eggshell and then rounding the pieces by rubbing them through a grooved stone. Megan Biesele learned that the originators of ostrich eggshell beadwork were people of 'an early race' who had gemsbok heads. In view of what we know about therianthropes (30, 31), this seems to be another link with the trance dance.

65b. Such a link is clear in a remarkable depiction of a secretary bird. It has a long spirit line from the top of its head (33) and two flywhisks (16d) apparently tucked under its wing. There can be little doubt that this bird is a shaman in avian form.

One of Wilhelm Bleek's /Xam men said that the shamans of a certain place were renowned for changing into birds: 'Yonder place at which //Kabbo lived, its sorcerers will turn themselves into birds.' In this form, a shaman is able to visit distant camps to find out how the people are faring:

Sometimes he sits on our heads; he sits peeping at us to see if we are still as we were when we left him. When he has seen that our hut is still nice, he flies away. As he flies away, he chirps, just as a little bird does when it flies away. We say to him, 'Return, for I knew it was you who had come to see me; I knew that it was not a little bird, but it was you.'

65a

Flight is, of course, a very widespread metaphor for trance experience because the sensations of rising up and floating that are part of many altered states of consciousness are produced by the universal human nervous system (23).

65c. It is probably in terms of these beliefs that other paintings and engravings of birds that do not have unusual features should be seen. Some of these birds are shown swooping down on animals or standing next to dead antelope.

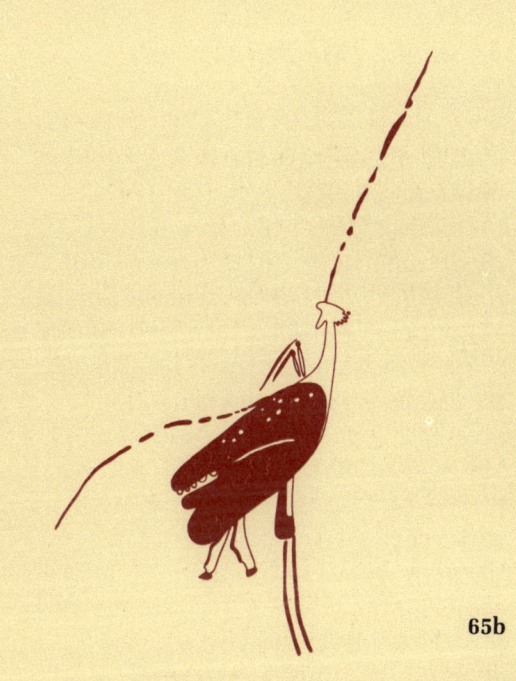

65b

65c

137

Elephant, rhinoceros, hippopotamus

66a. Elephants are fairly frequently painted and engraved. Paintings of them may be red, black or white; Bushman artists did not use colour realistically. Sometimes elephant are shown being hunted by a large party of men. Some of the most interesting paintings of elephants are in the western Cape. They are shown surrounded by zigzags and crenellated lines. Associated with these encircled elephants are therianthropes with elephant heads and trunks (31a). As Tim Maggs and Judy Sealy have suggested, the surrounding lines are almost certainly entoptic forms (25, 26, 27), and the elephants were thus part of a shaman's vision. Because these paintings are so like those of rain-animals in the Orange Free State (42-45), it may be that the western Cape Bushmen conceived of the rain-animal in the form of an elephant.

The !Kung, who categorise animals according to whether their meat is considered red, black or white (60), say that the elephant has all three types of meat in it. That is why it has remarkable potency. Megan Biesele tells of how they marvel at this fact after an elephant kill.

66b, c. Rhinoceros and hippopotamus are more common among the engravings than the paintings. Both the black and the white rhinoceros are represented. Some are so carefully and beautifully engraved that the folds of skin characteristic of these animals are depicted. There is no record of Bushman beliefs about these animals; all we can do is see them in the context of the art as a whole.

66a

66b

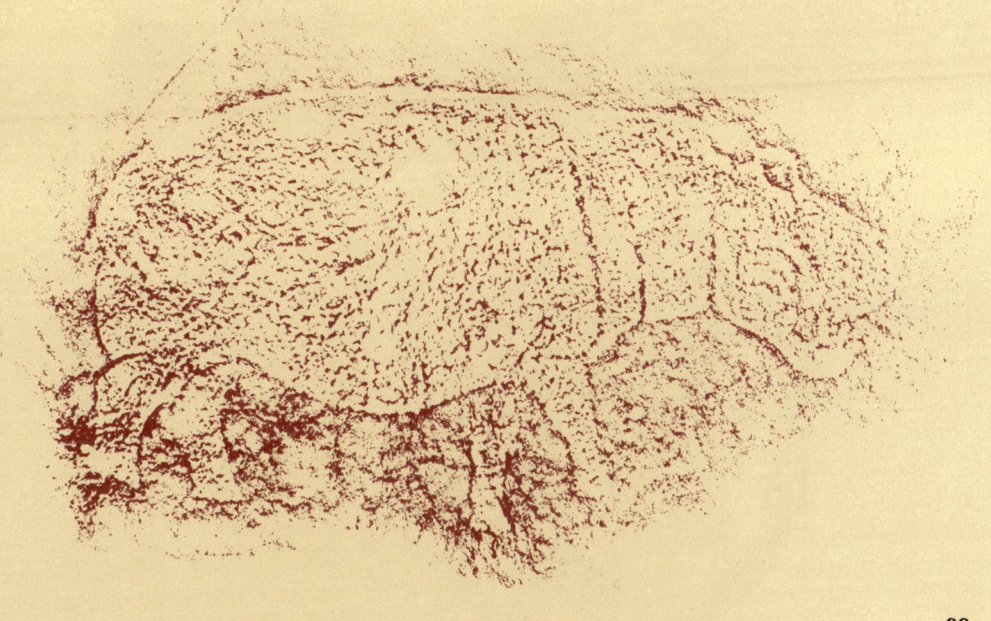

66c

139

Crabs

Occasionally, one finds a painting that is, as far as one knows, unique. The two crabs in **67a** are a case in point. Painted in black, they are almost surrounded by a thick line; above them are a number of bags (53b, d, 54).

To make interpretations more difficult, there are no recorded Bushman beliefs about crabs. Nevertheless, we can hazard an interpretation on the understanding that Bushman artists derived their subject matter from Bushman beliefs and that what they depicted fitted into the general artistic system, even if it was unique. Approached in this way, the unique crabs are fairly easily understood.

We have already seen that 'underwater' is a metaphor for trance experience (22) and that Bushman artists frequently suggested this metaphor by including fish in their compositions. Less frequently, they extended their 'underwater vocabulary' to include eels (22) and, in another unique painting, an artist depicted two turtles along with fish and eels (40). It will now be clear that the crabs, at first so puzzling, are in fact a unique extension of the 'underwater' metaphor.

If we are correct in this interpretation, we can move on to consider two further features of this interesting painting. First, the larger crab has clearly drawn pincers, but the smaller one has none. This

67a

67b

omission is explained by crab behaviour. They are territorial creatures and attack any other crab that intrudes on their preserve. In the fights that follow such intrusions, a crab may lose its pincers. In time, these will grow again. It seems, then, that we have here a large crab, still with its pincers, and a smaller crab that has been vanquished and that has lost its pincers in a territorial struggle.

The meaning of this significant detail is clear. If the crabs are indeed 'underwater' shamans, as the whole context of the art leads one to believe, they represent a battle in the spiritual realm in which one shaman has been overcome. The painting is thus akin to 63 where two shamans in the form of lions are being shot at by shamans in human form. Both paintings deal with supernatural conflict.

The second interesting feature of the painting is the thick, encircling line. At first one could suppose it to represent a pool, but very similar lines turn up in other contexts. Sometimes they seem to represent a hut circle or a rock shelter (**67b**) and, like the one around the crabs, are accompanied by bags or digging sticks. But in other cases they do not represent anything in the real world; the elephants in so-called boxes are examples (66a). At present we can go no further. All we can say is that, in the case of the crabs, the encircling line may not depict a pool and that, as research progresses, this remarkable painting may help to solve the problem of the encircling lines that appear in other contexts.

OTHER PEOPLES

About two thousand years ago, two new ways of life began to make themselves felt in southern Africa: pastoralism and farming. Then, just over three hundred years ago, white colonists began to settle in the subcontinent.

68a. Archaeological evidence shows that in the first couple of centuries of the Christian Era (C.E.), Khoikhoi pastoralists with their flocks of fat-tailed sheep were occupying the better grazing land along the southwest coast. It seems that, at the same time, the Bushmen of this region moved to the higher ground. There is some debate about the sharpness of the distinction between the Khoikhoi and the Bushmen. Both speak click languages, and there was probably some interchange of membership between the hunter-gatherers and the pastoralists.

At about the same time as the Khoikhoi were entering the western Cape, another way of life was taking root farther to the east. Most archaeologists believe that Negroid people speaking a Bantu language and practising farming gradually infiltrated the subcontinent about 1 800 years ago. Others believe that there were already some Negroid people in southern Africa who were

68a

hunters and gatherers. Either way, the first semipermanent villages with pottery, metals, crops and domesticated animals (**68b**) have been dated by radiocarbon to the third century C.E., but even earlier dates may still come to light. The gradual spread of the Iron Age, as this way of life is called, is shown on the accompanying map.

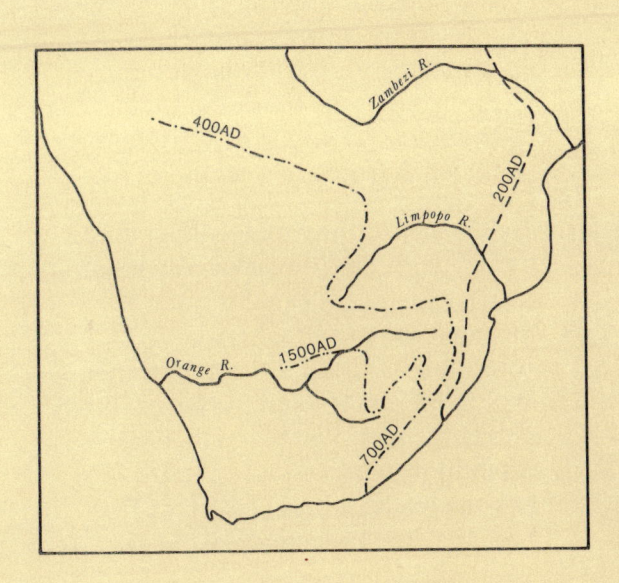

68b

Map showing the gradual spread of the Iron Age.

143

Archaeological evidence suggests that, from the earliest times, there was much contact between Iron Age farmers and Bushman hunter-gatherers. Client relationships developed in which Bushmen hunted and performed other tasks for Iron Age people who, in return, gave the Bushmen iron for arrow heads (52) and other rewards. By the middle of the nineteenth century this relationship was well developed. The Bushmen also became accepted as ritual specialists and made rain for Iron Age farmers. Some families went to live with chiefs as resident rain-makers. In times of stress, some Iron Age people fled into the mountains and lived with the Bushmen, to whom they were, in some cases, related. Although there were no doubt clashes from time to time, (69), a generally amicable relationship seems to have existed between the two groups until new tensions arose as new demands on the land and resources were made by white colonists.

The advance of the white colonists had far more serious repercussions for the Bushmen than either the Khoikhoi or the Iron Age people. The whites brought with them new diseases, guns, overgrazing of the veld and extermination of the vast herds of game. They saw the Bushmen as subhuman and set out to exterminate them. A British Government report of 1836 records the events of these terrible years in horrifying detail:

In 1774, an order was issued for the extirpation of the whole of the Bushmen, and three commandos, or military expeditions, were sent out to execute it. The massacre at that time was horrible, and the system of persecution continued unremitting, so that . . . it came to be considered a meritorious act to shoot a Bushman.

Under pressure, some Bushmen went to work for the white farmers. Another Government report (1863) records their fate:

Those who went into the service of the newcomers did not find their conditions thereby improved. Harsh treatment, and insufficient allowance of food, and continued injuries inflicted on their kinsmen are alleged as having driven them back into the bush, from whence hunger again led them to invade the flocks and herds of the intruders, regardless of the consequences, and resigning themselves, as they say, to the thought of being shot in preference to death from starvation.

By the end of the nineteenth century very few, if any, southern Bushmen still lived a traditional hunter-gatherer way of life. Many intermarried with the black farmers, but, to all intents and purposes, their end had come. To the north, other Bushman groups lived on in the less hospitable Kalahari Desert, as they had done for thousands of years.

The impact of the newcomers – Khoikhoi, Iron Age people and, most recently, the colonists – on Bushman rock art has been much discussed. There are some paintings that may depict Khoikhoi herders, but their presence in southern Africa is best shown by paintings of fat-tailed sheep (68a). These paintings are fairly common in the western Cape, but paintings of cattle, which the Khoikhoi also had, at least in more recent centuries, are generally absent. The eastern Cape, southern Natal and the eastern Orange Free State, however, have many paintings of cattle (68b). Often they are accompanied by Iron Age people carrying broad-bladed iron spears and shields. Sometimes these Iron Age people are depicted fighting against the Bushmen. The painting in 69 shows a seated Iron Age man with broad-bladed spears, a knobkierie and a Basotho shield. Bushmen with bows and arrows appear to be shooting at him.

69

70. Clashes with white colonists were also depicted. One of these paintings shows such details as horse bridles, flashes from rifles and even the flash from the pan of a flintlock rifle.

At first glance these paintings seem to be straightforward depictions of events that record violent skirmishes between Bushmen and other peoples. Indeed, they have played an important part in the theory that Bushman art is simply a narrative of daily events (p. 23-26). Recent research, however, has shown that there is more to these paintings than at first meets the eye. For instance, 69 includes a seated person in the hand-to-nose trance posture (19a). The colonists in **71** are surrounded by a non-realistic, convoluted line that also involves an ostrich (65a). The battle scene in 70, which includes cattle and fleeing Bushmen looking back over their shoulders, also has, to the right, a shaman bleeding from the nose (15) and with two long emanations from his head (33).

71

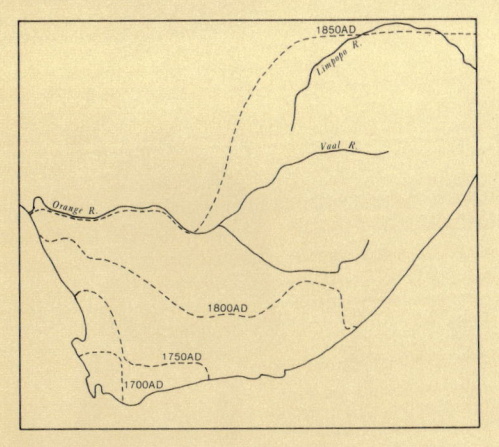

Map showing the advance of the white colonists

These features all point to shamanism and show that the new subject matter brought by the intruders was incorporated into the traditional shamanistic art. In more recent times the shamans used their supernatural powers to control and combat the newcomers even as, for centuries, they had used their powers to fight off malevolent shamans in the spirit world. There is also evidence that cattle and horses, and perhaps sheep as well, became symbols of potency and were used in the art of the final decades as eland and other animals had been used in earlier times.

COMPLEX PANELS

72. One of the most puzzling features of complex panels is superpositioning – the execution of one depiction on top of another. It is more common among paintings than among engravings. Sometimes one depiction overlaps another slightly; in other cases the second is done directly upon the first. At one time it was thought that superpositioning merely showed that artists did not take any notice of the work of their predecessors, but three discoveries challenged that explanation.

First, it was noticed that paintings are often superimposed even where there is plenty of clear rock face to accommodate a second depiction.

73

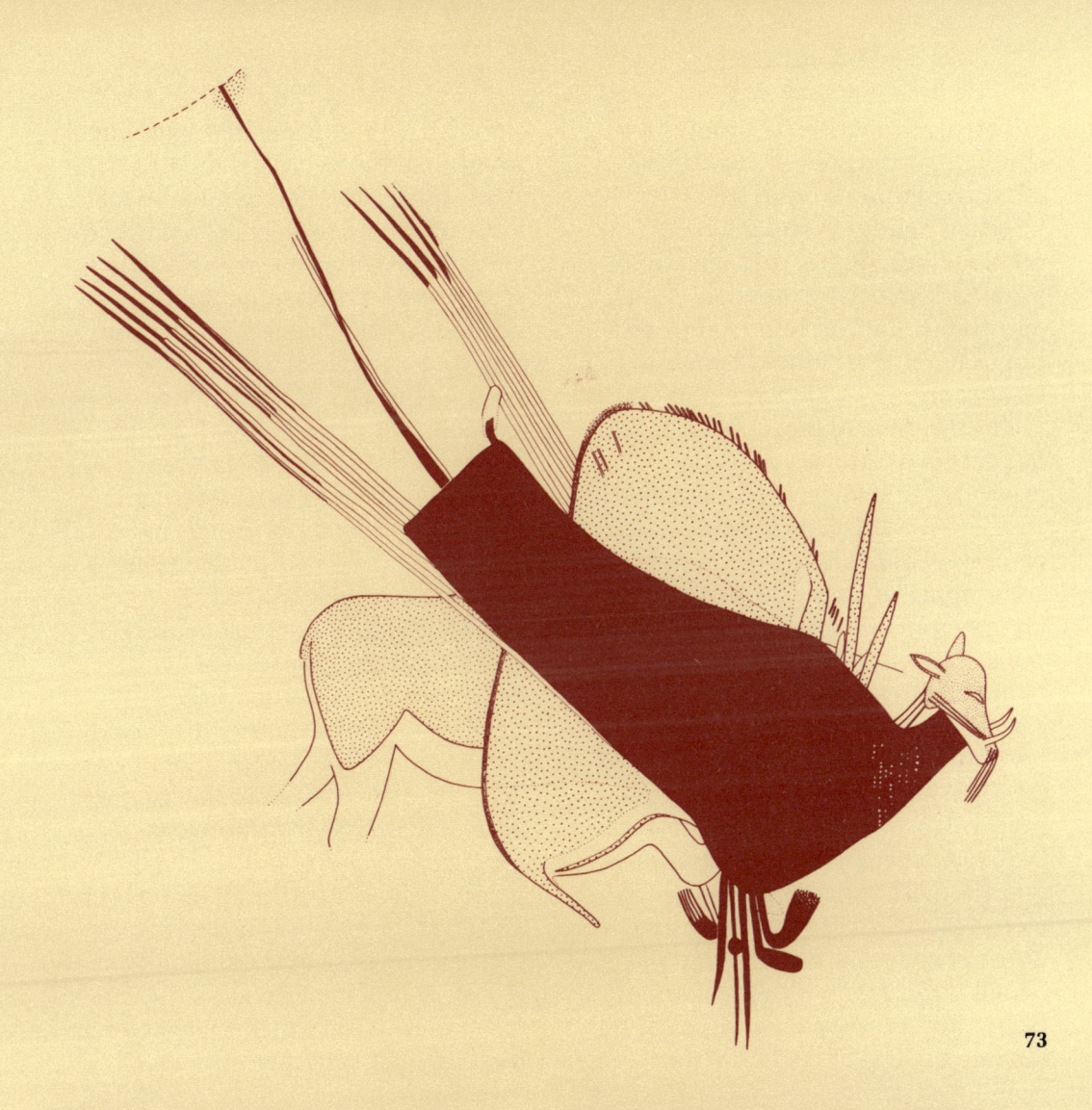

These cases suggest very strongly that the artist who made the second depiction deliberately placed it on top of the earlier one.

Secondly, there are cases of 'factitious superpositioning': an artist painted a depiction in two parts so that it appears to lie beneath another. In **73**, a hunting bag (53b) transformed into a trance-buck (32) was superimposed on a standing eland. Then a curled up, sleeping eland was painted in two parts to give the impression that it is under the trance-buck but on top of the standing eland. The sleeping eland was, as it were, slipped between the other two paintings. Clearly, the placing of one painting on top of another was important to the artist or artists who painted this combination.

Thirdly, quantitative studies have shown that the painters favoured certain combinations of superimposed paintings and avoided others. For instance, they frequently painted eland on top of other eland and eland on top of human figures, but they seldom painted human figures directly on top of eland.

The meaning of these patterns is not yet clear. All we can say at present is that superpositioning is consistent with shamanistic art. In trance vision, images are often superimposed on others. We have already noticed how entoptic forms are incorporated into images of animals (29) and people (35a, 38). The piling up of images, apparently without regard to any sort of relationship they may have in 'real' life, is also part of trance experience. Bushman shaman-artists who were familiar with trance experience would therefore not find anything unusual about the densely painted panels – especially if they regarded the paintings as visual images rather than depictions of real animals, people and events.

This explanation also clarifies why depictions are often painted next to one another in ways that one would not find in reality. For example, a group of human figures may be depicted walking along, apparently oblivious of a nearby elephant. Yet the artists do not appear to have been uncomfortable with these groupings. One explanation is that they automatically sorted out jumbled, complex panels, grouping paintings that belonged together. But what rules governed what belonged with what? Clearly, superpositioning shows that they observed rules that went beyond the perspective groupings that Westerners tend to impose on complex panels. It seems that they were intentionally painting associations of a kind with which Westerners are unfamiliar. Many of these associations derived from trance experience. In trance, highly improbable juxtapositionings are perfectly acceptable – as are combinations of human and animal characteristics (30, 31), the integration of entoptic forms with animals (29), and the superpositioning of one image upon another apparently completely unrelated image. In other words, complex panels are not 'compositions' as we may understand the term. Rather, they represent the 'feel' and essence of the shaman-artists' trance experience.

But these panels differ from Western art in another important way. Sometimes the older paintings are so faded that they are barely visible, while the more recent ones appear quite fresh. The reason for this is that people added their own contributions over extended periods of time. The panels are thus communally produced, pooled revelations of the spirit world, new insights and new power being contributed by a long line of artists. This pooling of spiritual experience is part of Bushman shamanism. During the trance dance, a shaman sometimes calls the attention of his fellow shamans to the visions he can see out in the darkness beyond the firelight. Then they too see the visions, and all the shamans are united and strengthened by their combined apprehension of the spirit world. It was therefore fitting for an artist to add in his or her contribution to a developing panel of revelations.

When looking at these panels, we should not waste too much time worrying about 'composition' and trying to sort out groups according to Western traditions. We should rather try to go beyond our Western limitations and attempt to absorb something of the complexity of the generations of insights and religious visions before us. Seen as accumulations of all the features we have explained, these panels can be overwhelming in their impact.

The principle that the whole of a Bushman rock panel is greater than a collection of individual depictions is well illustrated by **74**. This panel was

74

first copied by Elisabeth Mannsfeld, a member of the expedition that the German ethnographer Leo Frobenius brought to southern Africa during the years 1928-1930. Comparison of her copy with the panel as it is today shows that, although some figures have faded away completely, the greater understanding of Bushman rock art we now have enables us to decipher confused parts that were formerly baffling. For instance, there is, to the right, a buck-headed serpent bleeding from the nose (22, 62); Elisabeth Mannsfeld could not make it out. Similarly, Mannsfeld did not copy the strange crawling figure in the lowest part of the panel. Then, when it came to trying to understand the panel, the significance of figures such as the bending-forward and arms-back dancers (15, 17) must have escaped the copier. The important arms-back figure does not in fact appear in the early copy. On the other hand, the curious form with dots in the lower right remains enigmatic. The dots suggest some entoptic component, but there is nothing more we can say about it at present.

The overriding problem facing copiers like Mannsfeld, not to mention even earlier workers such as Stow and Orpen, was a lack of understanding of Bushman beliefs. They did not know that such apparently unrelated elements as certain human postures, animals and items of equipment were all part of a complex set of beliefs about shamans and their spiritual experiences. The unity of the art in general and the coherence of apparently jumbled panels were thus obscured.

Unlike the panel Mannsfeld copied, the panel in **75** has never been published. To the left there is a figure with raised knee (19c), and to the right a figure is in the arms-back posture (17). Neither is part of a 'dance scene', but each clearly refers to trancing. While these two figures depict trance dancing literally, a metaphor of trance has also been worked into the panel. To the left an eland bleeds from a number of

75

wounds, and to the right another is in the head-down dying posture (20, 21). A long kaross-clad figure holding a forked stick stands in front of the dying eland and is joined to it by a line. Unlike other lines, this one does not have white dots (41). To the left, there is a cluster of hunting bags with their shoulder straps looping over them (53b). The sets of small lines above each bag are probably the ends of link-shaft arrows (52), the white sections having faded. The hoofprints to the right are probably of eland (55-59); in another part of the panel (not shown here) there are small antelope prints, possibly rhebuck. The artists who built up this panel thus used symbols of potency (eland), metaphors of trance experience (death, bags), and significant postures (arms-back, knee raised).

When looking at this sort of combination of elements, we must put aside notions of perspective, vignettes of daily life and so forth. The dancing man superimposed on the wounded eland and the juxtaposed hunting bags, for instance, do not comprise a 'scene' taken from daily life. We should rather try to see different kinds of relationships. Perhaps the nearest we can come to grasping what is happening in Bushman rock art panels is to recall the use of pictures in advertisements. Often a product is placed next to a depiction with which it has no logical link. A sword-wielding Samurai warrior, for instance, may be associated with a pick-up truck. The combination allows the qualities of the Samurai to interact with the truck on a level far removed from daily life. In complex panels, the Bushman artists were similarly linking depictions so that they could interact on what we may call a symbolic level.

76-80. This kind of interaction is nowhere better seen than in the remarkable depictions with which we end our explanation of Bushman rock art. In addition to many of the features we have explained, these are highly unusual visions of the spirit world. We let them stand without detailed comment: they provide a challenge to the whole approach we have outlined. How much of the art is now within our understanding?

The complex depictions with which we have concluded this section bring together concepts that clearly confound the old ways of looking at Bushman rock art. There is no triviality here. Instead, there is a profound exploration by numerous shaman-artists of Bushman religious experience. Looking at the panels with some understanding of that experience, we may feel that we are just beginning to grasp some of the beliefs that, in Wilhelm Bleek's memorable phrase, 'most deeply moved the Bushman mind, and filled it with religious feelings'. Bushman rock art is indeed a remarkable monument to a people who suffered much and who continue to suffer at the hands of those who consider themselves superior.

76a and 76b combined to show the complete complex panel

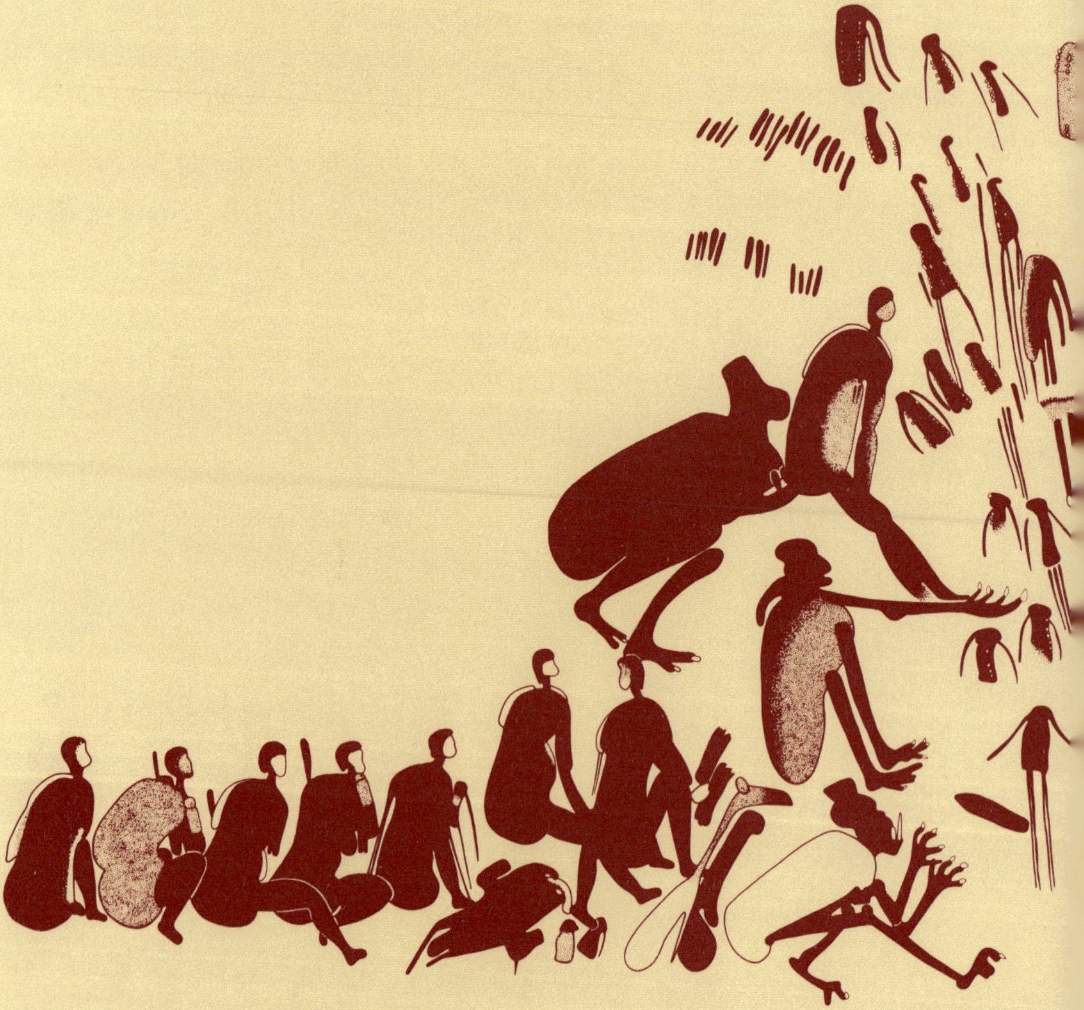

76a

158

76b

77

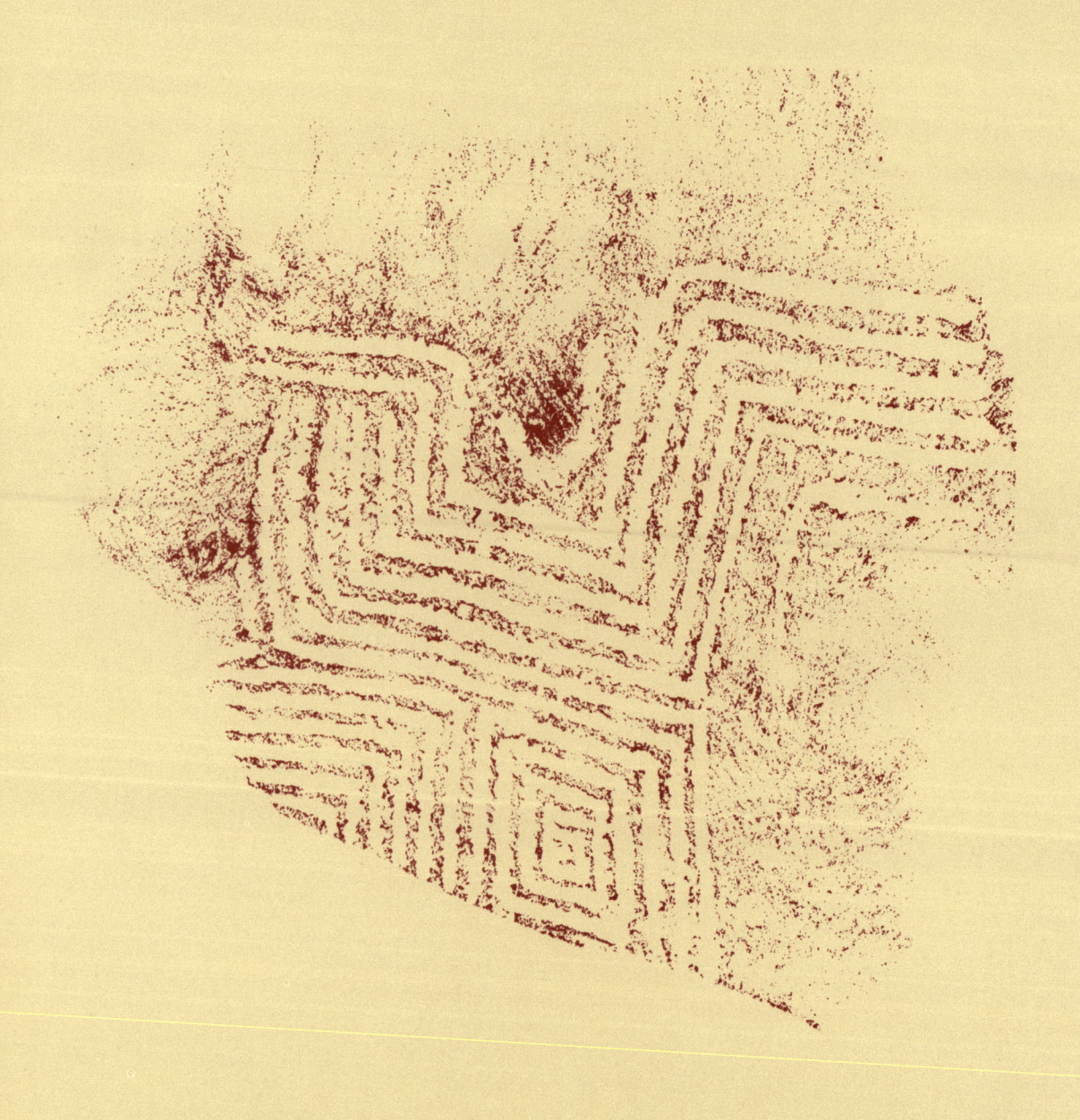

78

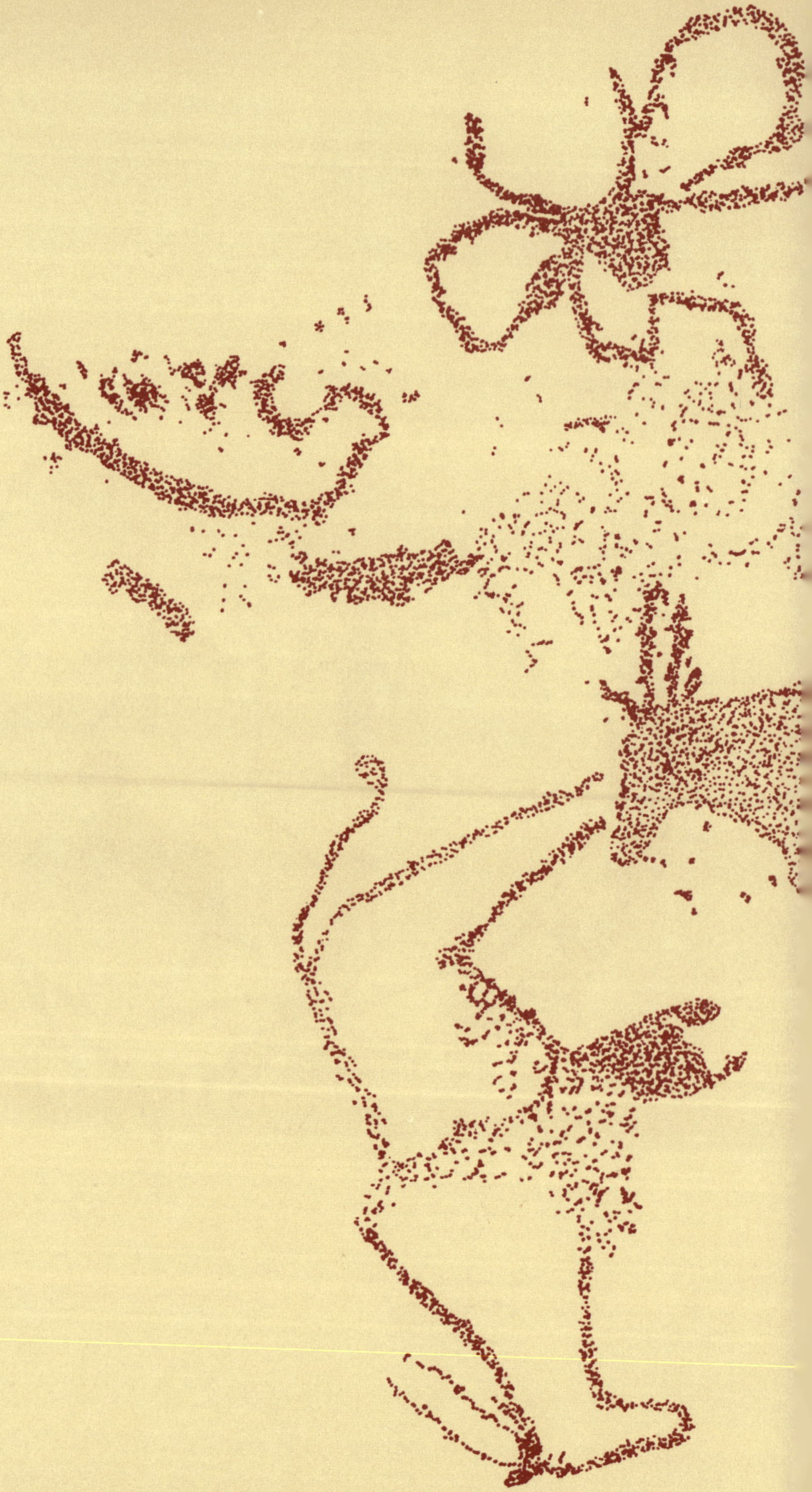

79

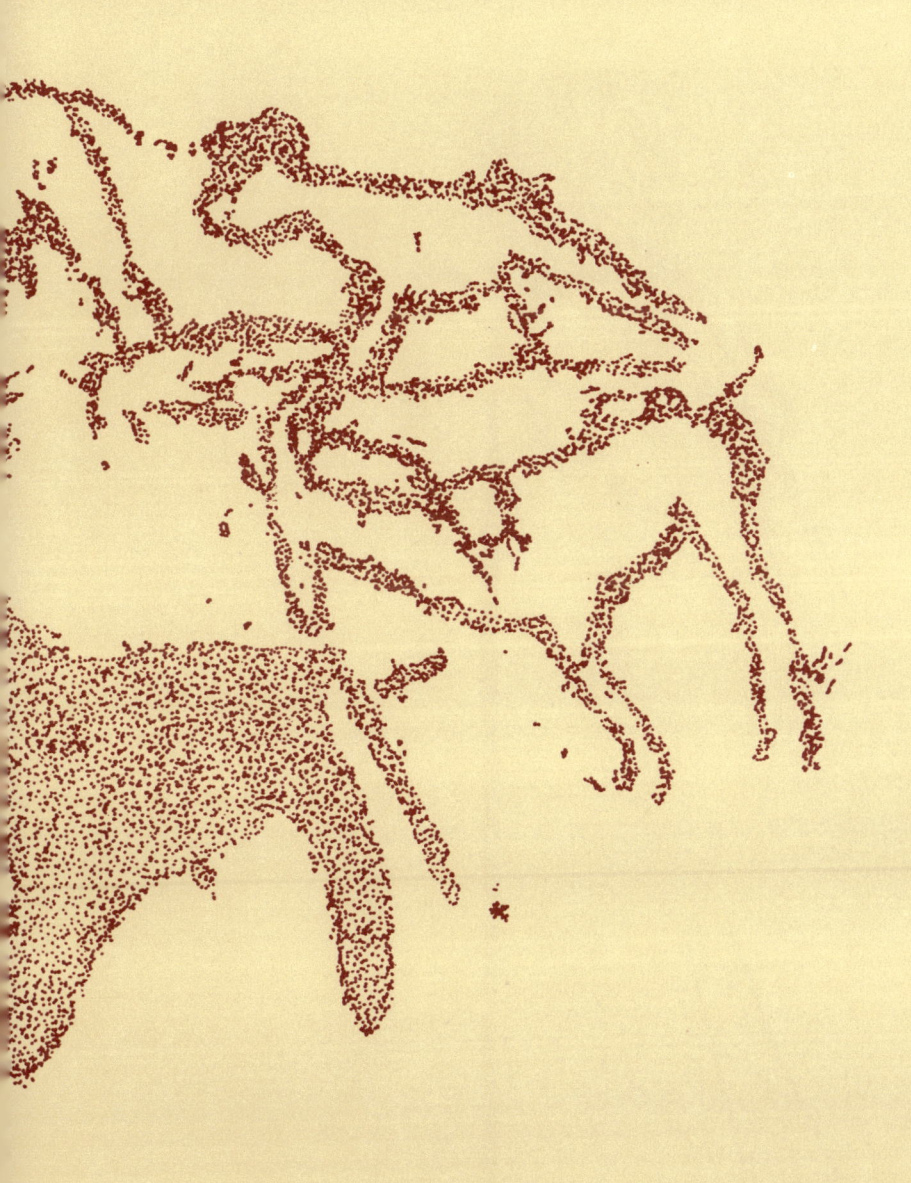

164

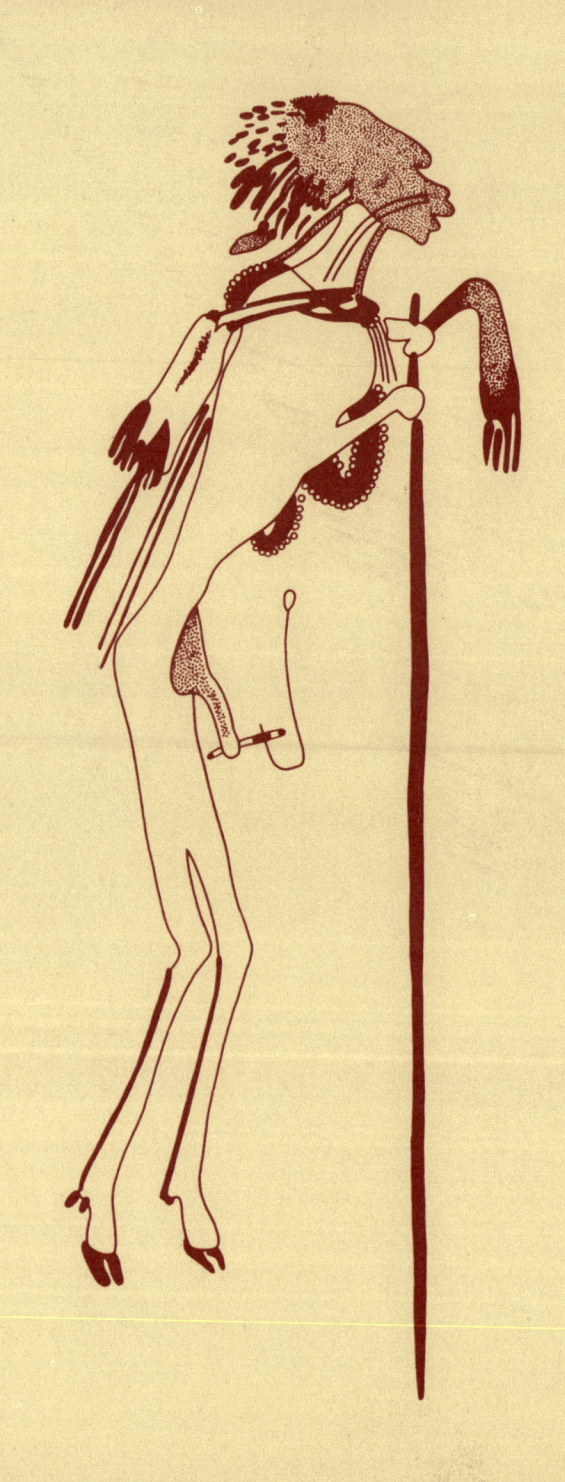

PART III

Artistic splendour

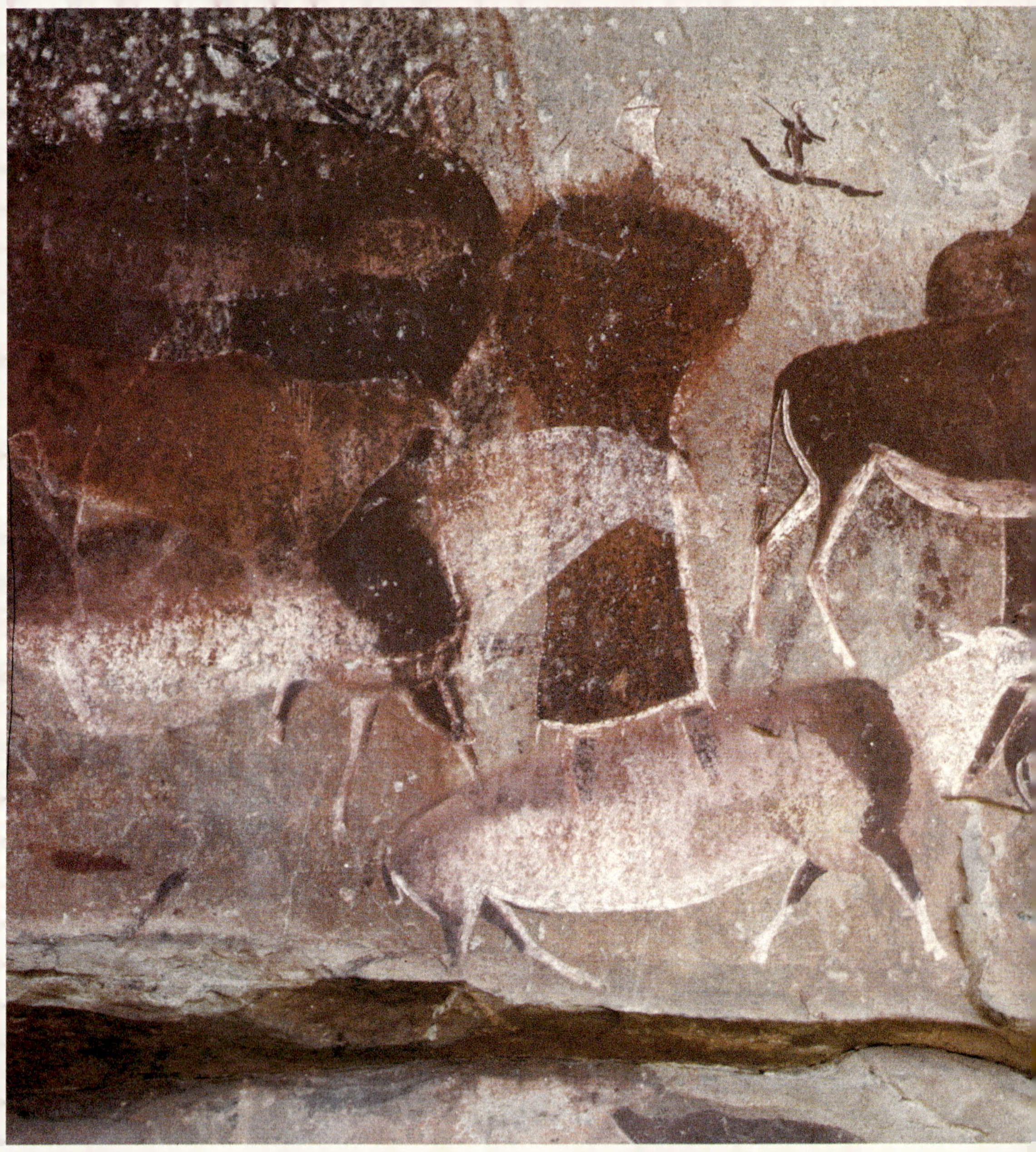

81 A well-preserved panel of polychrome eland and long kaross clad figures with hoofs. Smaller figures with bows are depicted running above the large paintings, and in the upper left part of the picture there are the remains of the shoulder, neck line and red forehead hair of a very large eland (Kamberg, Natal Drakensberg).

82a A well-preserved unshaded polychrome eland superimposed on the legs of an exceptionally large therianthrope. Two faded eland are above, and part of another therianthrope can be seen to the left (North-Eastern Cape).

82b A therianthrope with an antelope head. Note the dots on various parts of the painting (North-Eastern Cape).

82c Part of a large complex dance group. Note the ears and body markings (North-Eastern Cape).

83a Driekopseiland, a richly engraved glacial pavement in the northern Cape.

83b, c, d Details of the Driekopseiland engravings, showing various geometric forms. Pecked engravings.

84a A hallucinatory figure with animal head, and blood or foam falling from its mouth. It also has dots on its body and a line of dots coming from its neck (Natal Drakensberg).

84b A hallucinatory animal. Note the dots along its spine (Natal Drakensberg).

84c A hallucinatory figure holding a bow and arrows. Note the ears, whiskers and dots (Natal Drakensberg).

85a A large male polychrome eland (North-Eastern Cape).

85b The unique incised rock engraving of an eland with male and female features (Transvaal; scale in centimetres).

85c A scraped rock engraving of people surrounding an eland (Northern Karoo).

85d Two delicately painted rhebok (Natal Drakensberg).

85e Pecked rock engraving of the head of a hippopotamus (Transvaal).

85f The head of a sensitively painted shaded polychrome eland (East Griqualand, but now in Natal Museum, Pietermaritzburg).

85g The head of a bichrome feline leaping with outstretched front legs. Note the whiskers (Eastern Cape).

6a A dancing man with feathers or emanations from his head, and holding a knobbed stick (Natal Drakensberg).

86b A group of human figures painted in great detail (Eastern Orange Free State).

86c Painting of a trance experience. A feline leaps in the direction of two elongated human figures, one of whom is clapping. Above and to the right two figures somersault. Note the large number of red flecks scattered through the groups (Natal Drakensberg).

87a A fantastic, probably hallucinatory, bird connected to an eland by a line of supernatural potency that has a zigzag painted on it. Note that foam falls from the mouth of the polychrome eland to show that it is dying (North-Eastern Cape).

87b Painting of a monochrome kudu and other animals (Zimbabwe).

87c Painting of a monochrome bushpig (Natal Drakensberg).

87d Painting of a monochrome fish (Eastern Cape).

87e A trance hallucination of figures with fish or swallow tails. Note the long, attenuated figure (Southern Cape).

88a The Natal Drakensberg. There are many paintings in the large cave on the left.

88b Thomas Dowson tracing rock paintings in an eastern Cape site.

PART IV

Viewing the art

HOW TO VIEW THE ART

Rock art requires much closer viewing than many people imagine. Paintings, especially, cannot be appreciated by standing well away from the wall of the rock shelter as if one were viewing pictures in a gallery. The Mlambonja painting, for instance, measures only 5,5 cm from the tips of its horns to its feet (1). The viewer should therefore be as close to the rock face as the artist was when he or she painted it; only then can the exquisite details be seen. Even better is the use of a large magnifying glass. Many paintings spring to life when viewed through a lens. Often visitors to painted shelters are disappointed by the faintness of many paintings; but careful and well-informed examination will reveal much more than a distant, casual glance.

Never relinquish this kind of immediate scrutiny in favour of photography. Some students of the art spend all their time at a site feverishly photographing paintings in the belief that they will be able to study the photographs at leisure. Although photographs undeniably provide a record of certain photogenic paintings, they do not show very faint paintings or the minute, immaculate details that are the principal clues to the meaning of the paintings.

Moreover, the all-important relationships between depictions in large panels are obscured. Photography extracts especially striking paintings from complex panels, frames them, and then seems to invite comments from a Western point of view on what they depict and on their aesthetic merits. Indeed, photography, whatever its benefits, has been instrumental in the formulation of erroneous beliefs about Bushman rock art. Readers should therefore always bear in mind that most of the paintings selected for detailed explanation in Part II of this book have been extracted from larger compositions. Understanding these individual paintings is simply a prelude to looking at larger panels.

Knowing what to look for is as important as knowing how to look. We tend to see only what we expect to see. For instance, viewers who do not know about eared caps (46) or sectioned arrows (52) simply fail to notice them. Nor, unless they are prepared beforehand, do they see the tiny hairs on the Mlambonja creature. But familiarity with the detail of the art enables one often to reconstruct a panel so faded that most people would turn away from it disappointed. Experience also enables one to discern the faintest discoloration of the rock face where paint was formerly clearly visible. Clues such as the red patch of hair on an eland's forehead (55-59), missed by many people, will sometimes locate the head and thus enable one to make out the entire animal. Viewing rock art demands a fair amount of detective work, and very faded panels, useless for photography, are often the most interesting. Each figure should therefore be scrutinised for the details described in this book. The increased perception this practice brings will greatly enhance appreciation of the Bushman artists' meticulous work.

Time of day is another important factor in some shelters. Paintings invisible in the morning are sometimes discernible in the afternoon because the grain of the rock face is illuminated differently. Shading a painting with a hand often changes the angle of light and brings out a painting, even one already in shadow, much more clearly. Direct sunlight is seldom conducive to good viewing.

The angle of the sun is even more important when viewing rock engravings. Try shading apparently unengraved stones to see if a completely patinated depiction is present. If at all possible, visit a site in the morning and in the afternoon.

Remember:

- Never treat the rock with any substance whatsoever. Misguided beliefs about the application of water and other substances have destroyed and continue to destroy much of our art heritage.
- Do not touch the painted surfaces.
- Do not chip, scratch or stand on engraved rocks.
- Never make fires in a painted shelter or next to engraved rocks.
- Never scribble or write your name on or anywhere near painted and engraved surfaces.
- Never try to 'touch up' the paintings or enhance the engravings.
- Never try to remove paintings or engravings.
- Report any cases of damage to the police.
- Make sure that you know who visits art sites if you have any on your property. Always accompany visitors to sites.
- The National Monuments Act (No. 28 of 1969 as amended by No. 13 of 1981) protects all ancient sites and states that:

No person shall destroy, damage, excavate, alter, remove from its original site or export from the Republic any drawing or painting on stone or a petroglyph known or commonly believed to have been executed by any other people who inhabited the Republic before the settlement of the Europeans at the Cape.

Anyone who contravenes this law is liable to a fine of up to R5 000 or imprisonment of up to 12 months, or both.

The best-preserved paintings are those that are seldom visited. Repeated wetting an touching of paintings fade the paint rapidly.

WHERE TO VIEW THE ART

The painted rock shelters and the open engraving sites have an ambience that no museum exhibit or book can possibly capture. Every effort should therefore be made to visit sites open to the public. Sites on private property should not be visited without the owner's permission. At all times the rules given above should be strictly observed.

The remoteness of many sites makes it impossible for some people to see the art in its natural surroundings. Fortunately, numerous museums in southern Africa have collections of paintings and engravings. All the collections are interesting, but those at the South African Museum (Cape Town), the Africana Museum (Johannesburg), the McGregor Museum (Kimberley) and the National Cultural History Museum (Pretoria) rank among the most important rock art collections in the world and should on no account be missed.

SITES OPEN TO THE PUBLIC

Unfortunately, the appalling vandalism that has damaged and in some cases destroyed so many sites makes it no longer advisable to reveal the exact locations of sites that are not adequately protected. Even in the scientific literature it is no longer customary to give the exact locations of sites. The numbers of illustrations taken from the following sites are given in brackets.

BOTSWANA

Francistown
There are several rock painting sites in the eastern part of the country, but most sites have few paintings and are often difficult to find. Directions can be obtained from the National Museum, Gaborone, but visitors also require permission from the landowners or tribal authorities.

Manyana
There are about 27 surviving paintings scattered along a low south-facing ridge; they occur in five sets spread over about 750 metres. Manyana is about 50 km south of Gaborone. Detailed directions can be obtained from the National Museum in Gaborone.

Matsieng
There are several rock engraving sites in southeast Botswana, of which Matsieng is the best known and most accessible. The site is near the Gaborone-Mahalapye road, 43 km from Gaborone. Detailed directions can be obtained from the National Museum, Gaborone.

Tsodilo
The paintings in the Tsodilo Hills are the best-known rock art sites in Botswana, but they are also the most difficult to reach. They are several hundred kilometres from Maun. The

hills rise sharply from the flat, sandy Kalahari and have a very special ambience. Visitors can now fly in by a light aeroplane, but the hills are about 10 km long and a fourwheel-drive vehicle allows greater mobility once there. Visitors must take their own water. Detailed directions can be obtained from the National Museum, Gaborone.

LESOTHO

Lesotho is one of the richest sources of rock paintings in southern Africa. Enquiries at villages and towns usually lead to sites, but permission must always be obtained from the local authorities. There are a number of well-known sites near Maseru.

NAMIBIA

The Brandberg (2)
This mountain massif is known especially for the so-called White Lady, but there are many other sites. The White Lady, or Maack, Shelter is in the Tsisab Valley and is easily reached from the Uis-Khorixas road, but detailed directions should be obtained from the State Museum in Windhoek.

The Erongo Mountains
On the northern side of the mountains, a number of sites may be reached from the Etemba guest farm, where permission should also be obtained. On the southern side, the farms Ameib, Onguati and David Ost can be reached from the Usakos-Okombahe road. Permission should be sought at the farms.

The Spitzkoppe
This area can be reached from the Usakos-Swakopmund road and is well signposted. The paintings, much damaged by vandalism, are in small groups scattered around the mountain.

Twyfelfontein
This site, which is well known for its many rock engravings, is most easily reached from Khorixas or from the Uis-Khorixas road. Guides are available.

SOUTH AFRICA

Cape Province

Ceres Nature Reserve
Path to paintings is signposted. Permission to visit the site may be obtained at the Nature Reserve office.

Dinorbin
This farm is about 20 minutes' drive from Barkly East on the Elliot road. There is a fine collection of rock paintings; the higher ones are better preserved and reward close attention. The owners of the farm have constructed an approach to the art and provide a tape-recorded commentary. Appointments to see the art can be made by contacting Mr and Mrs Small, Dinorbin, Barkly East.

Driekopseiland (near Kimberley)
A remarkable rock engraving site in a riverbed. Directions may be obtained at the McGregor Museum, Kimberley.

Elephant Cave, Kromrivier (also known as Stadsaal Cave)
As the name implies, this site is characterised by striking depictions of elephants, but there are other interesting paintings. Permission to view the art can be obtained at Kromrivier Farm. Take the Algeria turn-off from the N7. The farm is about 25 km from the Algeria forest station. There is an entrance fee.

Kalkoenkranz
This site is about 20 minutes' drive from Aliwal North. It contains an exceptionally varied, interesting and well-preserved collection of paintings. One of the panels in the main shelter has an unusually diverse set of paintings of animals. Access to the site is permitted only in the company of a guide. Application should be made in advance to The Manager, Hot Springs, Aliwal North.

Martinshoek (55a, 65c)
This site is about 10 minutes' drive from Rhodes. A signpost on the Barkly East road indicates a side road. There is a picnic area from which the steep ascent to the shelter can be begun. The paintings are so remarkably well preserved that it has been suggested that they have been touched up. The site has been fenced to prevent vandalism.

Natal

Battle Cave, Injasuti (19c, 33b, 47b)
Permission to visit this large and interesting site may be obtained at the Natal Parks Board Injasuti camp. Visitors to the site must be accompanied by a Parks Board guide. It is about a two-hour walk from the camp. Chalets may be reserved at the camp. Telephone: Natal Parks Board, 0331-51514.

Game Pass, Kamberg (20, 35b, 48a, 72, 81)
This dramatic site contains some of the best-preserved paintings in southern Africa. The steep climb to the site takes just over an hour. The site is fenced and the Natal Parks Board does not permit entrance without a guide. Visits to the site may be undertaken on Sundays only. Chalets may be reserved at the rest camp. Telephone: Natal Parks Board, 0331-51514.

Main Caves, Giant's Castle (31c, 60a)
This is one of the biggest and best-preserved painted sites in southern Africa. If only one site can be visited, it should be Main Caves. There is a site museum and a tape-recorded commentary. The site is an easy 30-minute walk from the Natal Parks Board camp. There is an entrance fee.

Chalets may be reserved by telephoning the Parks Board: 0331-51514.

Orange Free State

Modderpoort
This site is behind the Modderpoort religious settlement, about 20 minutes' drive north from Ladybrand. Because the public has had unrestricted access to it for many years, the paintings are poorly preserved.

Schaapplaats
This site, a few kilometres outside Clarens on the Fouriesburg road, has some interesting therianthropes. Permission to visit the site must be obtained from the owner of the farm.

Transvaal

Gold River Ranch, Waterberg
There are a number of interesting sites in this private game reserve. For details of admission and accommodation, telephone 011-8271845.

Kruger National Park
There are many sites in the southern part of the park. A Bushman Trail takes visitors to a number of sites. For details of admission and accommodation, write to National Parks Board, P.O. Box 787, Pretoria, 0001.

Lapalala Wilderness (60b)
There are a number of sites in this beautiful area of the Waterberg. For details of admission and accommodation, write to Wilderness Trust, P.O. Box 577, Bedfordview, 2008.

SWAZILAND

There are numerous sites with well-preserved paintings in Swaziland. Directions to them can be obtained from the Museum in Mbabane.

ZIMBABWE

Nswatugi, Matopo Hills
Seven kilometres from Maleme Dam, on a park road leading to the Antelope Road, a signpost indicates the turn-off to this large and densely painted site.

Silozwane, Matopo Hills
South of the Matopos National Park. Enquire for detailed directions at the Park.

Diana's Vow (170 km from Harare or 71 km from Inyanega)
Detailed directions to the site may be obtained from the National Museum, Harare, or from Inyanega National Park.
Directions to many other sites in Zimbabwe are given in Peter Garlake's book *The painted caves: an introduction to the prehistoric art of Zimbabwe*.

MUSEUMS WITH ROCK ART COLLECTIONS

(The numbers of illustrations taken from rock art in the following institutions are given in brackets.)

Cape Province

South African Museum, Cape Town (22, 35c, 36b, 36c, 49a)
This museum houses the most important collection of rock art in any institution in southern Africa. The collection, comprising paintings and engravings, includes the famous Linton and Zaamenkomst panels, which were removed from sites in the eastern Cape at the beginning of the century.

McGregor Museum, Kimberley
The museum houses a comprehensive collection of rock engravings.

Natal

Natal Museum, Pietermaritzburg
There is a small but fine collection of rock paintings in this museum, including the well-known panel of polychrome eland from The Meads and the large Bamboo Mountain rain-animal scene.

Local History Museum, Durban
A small but interesting collection.

Orange Free State

National Museum, Bloemfontein (43)
The collection in this museum includes paintings removed from a number of sites in the eastern Orange Free State.

Transvaal

Africana Museum, Johannesburg (38a, 38b, 71)
There is an interesting collection of rock paintings in the museum. Some, removed from sites in the eastern Cape, are remarkably detailed.

National Cultural History Museum, Pretoria
This museum houses a very large collection of rock engravings. The exhibit has ten engravings on display; the others may be viewed by arrangement with the Director.

The Zoo, Johannesburg (60c, 64b, 66c)
One of the finest collections of rock engravings is laid out in an attractive open-air setting.

SUGGESTIONS FOR FURTHER READING

I. Books on southern African rock art

Fock, G.J. 1979. *Felsbilder in Südafrika (Teil I)*. Köln: Böhlau Verlagsanstalt.

Fock, G.J. and D. Fock. 1984. *Felsbilder in Südafrika (Teil II)*. Köln: Böhlau Verlagsanstalt.

Garlake, P. 1987. *The painted caves: an introduction to the prehistoric art of Zimbabwe*. Harare: Modus Publications.

Johnson, T. and T.M. O'C. Maggs. 1979. *Major rock paintings of southern Africa*. Cape Town: David Philip.

Lewis-Williams, J.D. 1981. *Believing and seeing: symbolic meanings in southern San rock paintings*. London: Academic Press.

Lewis-Williams, J.D. 1983. *The rock art of southern Africa*. Cambridge: Cambridge University Press.

Lewis-Williams, J.D. (Ed.) 1983. *New approaches to southern African rock art*. Goodwin Series 4. Cape Town: South African Archaeological Society.

Pager, H. 1971. *Ndedema*. Graz: Akademische Druck Verlagsanstalt.

Vinnicombe, P. 1976. *People of the eland*. Pietermaritzburg: Natal University Press.

II. Books about the Bushmen

How, M.W. 1962. *The mountain Bushmen of Basutoland*. Pretoria: Van Schaik.

Katz, R. 1982. *Boiling energy: community healing among the Kalahari !Kung*. Cambridge, Mass.: Harvard University Press.

Lee, R.B. 1984. *The Dobe !Kung*. New York: Holt, Rinehart and Winston.

Marshall, J. and C. Ritchie, 1984. *Where are the Ju/wasi of Nyae Nyae?* Cape Town: Centre for African Studies, University of Cape Town.

Marshall, L. 1976. *The !Kung of Nyae Nyae*. Cambridge, Mass.: Harvard University Press.

Shostak, M. 1981. *Nisa: the life and words of a !Kung woman*. Cambridge, Mass.: Cambridge University Press.

Thomas, E. Marshall. 1988. *The harmless people*. Cape Town: David Philip.

Tobias, P.V. (Ed.) 1978. *The Bushmen*. Cape Town: Human and Rousseau.

Wannenburgh, A., P. Johnson and A. Bannister. 1979. *The Bushmen*. Cape Town: Struik.

Wright, J.B.C. 1971. *Bushman raiders of the Drakensberg*. Pietermaritzburg: University of Natal Press.

SOME OTHER WORKS CITED IN THIS BOOK

Arbousset, T. and F. Daumas. 1846. *Narrative of an exploratory tour of the north-east of the Cape of Good Hope.* Cape Town: Robertson. (Reprint 1968, Cape Town: Struik)

Biesele, M. 1978. Sapience and scarce resources: communication systems of the !Kung and other foragers. *Social Science Information* 17: 921-947.

Biesele, M. 1979. Old K"xau. In J. Halifax (Ed.) *Shamanistic voices.* New York: Dutton, pp. 54-62.

Bleek, D.F. 1924. *The Mantis and his friends.* Cape Town: Maskew Miller.

Bleek, D.F. 1931. Customs and beliefs of the /Xam Bushmen. Part I: Baboons. *Bantu Studies* 5: 167-179.

Bleek, D.F. 1932. Customs and beliefs of the /Xam Bushmen. Part II: The lion; Part III: Game animals; Part IV: Omens, wind-making, clouds. *Bantu Studies* 6: 47-63, 233-249, 321-342.

Bleek, D.F. 1933. Beliefs and customs of the /Xam Bushmen. Part V: The Rain; Part VI: Rain-making. *Bantu Studies* 7: 297-312, 375-392.

Bleek, D.F. 1935. Beliefs and customs of the /Xam Bushmen. Part VII: Sorcerors. *Bantu Studies* 9: 1-47.

Bleek, D.F. 1936. Beliefs and customs of the /Xam Bushmen. Part VIII: More about sorcerors and charms. *Bantu Studies* 10: 131-162.

Bleek, W.H.I. and L.C. Lloyd. 1911. *Specimens of Bushman folklore.* London: Allen. (Reprint 1968, Cape Town: Struik)

Breuil, H. 1955. *The White Lady of the Brandberg.* London: Trianon Press.

Cameron, T. and S.B. Spies (Eds). 1986. *An illustrated history of South Africa.* Johannesburg: Jonathan Ball.

Campbell, C. 1986. Images of war: a problem in San rock art research. *World Archaeology* 18: 255-268.

Deacon, J. 1986. 'My place is the Bitterpits': the home territory of Bleek and Lloyd's /Xam San informants. *African Studies* 45: 135-155.

Deacon, J. 1988. The power of a place in understanding southern San rock engravings. *World Archaeology* 20: 129-140.

Deacon, H.J., J. Deacon and M. Brooker. 1976. Four painted stones from Boomplaas Cave, Oudtshoorn district. *South African Archaeological Bulletin* 31: 141-145.

Dowson, T.A. 1988. Revelations of religious reality: the individual in San rock art. *World Archaeology* 20: 116-128.

Guenther, M.G. 1986. 'San' or 'Bushmen'? In M. Biesele, R. Gordon and R. Lee (Eds): *The past and future of !Kung ethnography: critical reflections and symbolic perspectives.* Hamburg: Helmut Buske Verlag, pp. 27-51.

Jolly, P. 1986. A first-generation

descendant of the Transkei San. *South African Archaeological Bulletin* 41: 6-9.

Lewis-Williams, J.D. 1974. Superpositioning in a sample of rock paintings from the Barkly East district. *South African Archaeological Bulletin* 29: 93-103.

Lewis-Williams, J.D. 1982. The economic and social context of southern San rock art. *Current Anthropology* 23: 429-449.

Lewis-Williams, J.D. 1986. The last testament of the southern San. *South African Archaeological Bulletin* 41: 10-11.

Lewis-Williams, J.D. and T.A. Dowson. 1988. The signs of all times: entoptic phenomena in Upper Palaeolithic art. *Current Anthropology* 29: 201-245.

Maggs, T.M. O'C. and J. Sealy. 1983. Elephants in boxes. *Goodwin Series* 4: 44-48.

Manhire, T., J. Parkington and R. Yates. 1985. Nets and fully recurved bows: rock paintings and hunting methods in the western Cape, South Africa. *World Archaeology* 17: 161-174.

Marshall, L. 1969. The medicine dance of the !Kung Bushmen. *Africa* 39: 347-381.

Mazel, A.D. 1982. Principles for conserving the archaeological resources of the Natal Drakensberg. *South African Archaeological Bulletin* 37: 7-15.

Orpen, J.M. 1874. A glimpse into the mythology of the Maluti Bushmen. *Cape Monthly Magazine* (N.S.) 9: (49) 1-13.

Potgieter, E.F. 1955. *The disappearing Bushmen of Lake Chrissie.* Pretoria: van Schaik.

Reichel-Dolmatoff, G. 1978. *Beyond the Milky Way: hallucinatory imagery of the Tukano Indians.* Los Angeles: UCLA Latin America Centre.

Rudner, I. 1983. Paints of the Khoisan rock artists. *Goodwin Series* 4: 14-20.

Siegel, R.K. 1977. Hallucinations. *Scientific American* 237: 132-140.

Thackeray, A.I., J.F. Thackeray, P.B. Beaumont and J.C. Vogel. 1981. Dated rock engravings from Wonderwerk Cave, South Africa. *Science* 214: 64-67.

Van der Merwe, N.J., J. Sealy and R. Yates. 1987. First accelerator carbon-14 date for pigment from a rock painting. *South African Journal of Science,* 33: 56-57.

Wendt, W.E. 1976. 'Art mobilier' from the Apollo 11 Cave, South West Africa: Africa's oldest dated works of art. *South African Archaeological Bulletin* 31: 5-11.

Willcox, A.R. 1984. *The rock art of Africa.* Johannesburg: Macmillan.

Yates, R., J. Golson and M. Hall. 1985. Trance performance: the rock art of Boontjieskloof and Sevilla. *South African Archaeological Bulletin* 40: 70-80.

INDEX

Africana Museum, 84, 188
age of art, 20-23
   by radiocarbon dating, 21, 143
Aliwal North, 186
Altamire, 23
amino acids, 19
animal behaviour, 50, 52, 54, 57, 58, 86, 119, 141
animal incantations, 118
Apollo 11 cave, 21
   rock art from, **8**, 22
aprons, 105
Arbousset, T., 126
arms-back, *see* postures
aromatic herbs, *see* buchu
arrows, 7, 38, 50, 58, 70, 100, 104, 112, 127, 145, 154, **3, 84b, 85c**
   mystical, 38, 44, 48, 70, 129, 133, 135, **14**
art-for-art's sake, 24
art regions, 16-18
artists, identity of, 4-8
Asclepia gibba, 19

baboon, 134-135, **65a**
bags, 114, 116, 134, 140, 149, 154
   depictions of, **53b, 53d, 54, 67a, 75, 76a**
bangles, 106
Banisteriopsis, 60
Bantu languages, 9, 11, 142
   speakers, *see* Iron Age farmers
Barkly East, 185, 186
Barnard, A., 28
bees, 34, 63, 64
   depictions of, **27a, 28, 45**
bending forward, *see* postures
Biesele, M., 11, 28, 34, 54, 106, 118, 122, 126, 127, 136, 138
birds, 56, 85, 86, 136-137
   depictions of, **23, 38b, 39a, 65b, 65c, 87a**
Bleek, D.F., 134
Bleek, W.H.I., 26, **10**, 28-30, 40, 46, 54, 69, 92, 98, 100, 106, 108, 118, 120, 136, 155
Bloemfontein, 188
blood, 19, 36, 44, 59, 94, **75**
   nasal, 40, 49, 52, 63, 64, 72, 78, 80, 86, 88, 94, 128, 130, 147, 152, **15, 17, 18, 19b, 22, 24, 28, 30a, 32, 33b, 35a, 36, 39a, 40, 41a, 47a, 62, 63, 70, 72, 73, 80**
Boomplaas cave, 21
bored stones, 114, 116, **53e, 54**

Botswana, 8, 184
bow, 7, **3**, 48, 100, 112, 119, 135, 145
   depictions of, **2, 19a, 28, 34a, 46, 51, 52, 54, 63, 69, 73, 75, 84b, 85c, 86b**
Brandberg, 6, 14, 185
Breuil, H., 6, 7, 25
buchu, 35, 94
Bushmen
   chiefs, 12
   early opinions of, 4
   egalitarianism, 12, 31
   ethnography, 26-30
   genetic characteristics, 9
   languages, 11, 12, 142
   myths, 13, 29, 54, 116, 120, 125, 126, 128, 129, 130, 131, 135
   religion, 13, 34, 35, 36, 54, 126
   way of life, 11-12
   words used for, 8-9
bushpig, **87c**

canna, *see* dagga
Cape Province, 8, 17, 104, 108, 136, 138, 145, 188
Cape Town, 26, 188
caps, 75, 100, 129
   with ears, depictions of, **16d, 17, 24, 28, 41a, 45, 46, 82c**
cation-ratio dating of rock art, 22
cattle, 8, 9, 142-147
   depictions of, **68b, 70**
caves, *see* rock shelters
Cedarberg, 14
Ceres Nature Reserve, 185
chameleon, 117
charcoal, 18, 19
clapping, 31, 38, 42, 46, 105
   depictions of, **16a, 28, 67b, 76a, 86c**
clay, 18, 19
clicks, linguistic, 11, 142
clothing, 106
   see also apron, kaross
colonists, 4, 12, 112, 144-147
   depictions of, **70, 71**
colours in rock paintings, 7, 8, 120
   bichrome, 17, 22
   monochrome, 16, 22
   polychrome, 17, 22, 120
commandos, 144, 147
construals, 63-64, 67

192

control of animals, *see* shamans
crabs, 140
    depictions of, 35, **67a**
cracks, in rock face, 88, 90, 130
curing rituals, *see* shamans and trancedance

dagga, 130
dances, 8, 29, 30, 31, 51, 64, 94, 105, 117, 150, **12, 13, 82c, 86a**
    depictions of, 8, 28, 29, 104, **14, 15, 17, 18**
dancing rattles, 32, 44, 129, **15, 17**
dancing sticks, 40, 44, **15, 17, 19b, 20, 28, 38, 67b, 70**
dating rock art, *see* age of art
Daumas, F., 126
Deacon, H. and J., 21
death
    of eland, 50-51
    as metaphor, *see* metaphors
dewlap, 122
Diä!kwain, 98
diamonds, 20
Diamphidia simplex, 112
diffusion of art, 21-22
digging sticks, 105, 114, 116, 117, **53e, 54**
Dinorbin, 185
disease, 144
distribution of rock art, 13-18, **4**
domestic animals, *see* cattle, ox, sheep
Dorn, R., 22
Dornan, S., 134
dots, *see* entoptic phenomena
Drakensberg, 3, 11, 14, 17, 21, 36, 48, 104, 116, 136, **88a**
Draper, P., 28
dreams, 31, 35, 94
Driekopseiland, **83a**, 186
drought, 11
drum dance, 46-47
Durban, 188

ears, 85, 100
eels, 55, 88, 140, **22, 40**
eggwhite, 19
eland, 13, 19, 29, 30, 34, 36, 51, 66, 80, 90, 94, 118-125
    depictions of, 17, 18, 108, 149, **15, 20, 21a, 21c, 22, 24, 29, 35b, 37b, 41a, 41b, 55, 56, 57, 58, 59, 65c, 72, 73, 74, 75, 79, 81, 82a, 85a, 85b, 85c, 85f, 87a**
Eland Bull Dance, 105, 119
elephant, 7, 138, **66a**
Elephant Cave, 186

elongation, *see* hallucination, somatic
entoptic phenomena, 22, 60-67, 78, 84, 87, 94, 95, 101, 108, 133, 138, 150, 152, **25, 26, 84a, b, c,**
    depictions of, **17, 25, 26, 27a, 27b, 29, 30c, 32d, 35c, 39, 42, 43, 46, 48b, 63, 71, 77, 78, 83b, c, d, 86c**
equipment, 112-117
Erongo Mountains, 185

faces, 106-107
fat, 19, 70, 118, 119, 122
feathers, 57, 116, **86a**
    as brushes, 19
felines, 22, 34, 46, 70, 132-133, 135
    depictions of, 22, 25, **63, 85g, 86c**
ferric oxide, 18
fights, 24, 110
    between animals, 58, 141, **24**
    between people, **51**
fire, 31
first-kill rituals, 102, 118-119, 126
fish, 55, 57, 86, 140
    depictions of, **22, 23, 39a, 87d**
    see also metaphors, underwater
flecks, *see* entoptic phenomena
flight, *see* metaphors, flight
Florisbad skull, 9
flywhisk, 43, 55, 72, 88, 104, 136
    depictions of, **16d, 18, 22, 32c, 35c, 40, 65b, 73, 80**
Font-de-Gaume, 23
foreigners in the art, 4, 6, 8
Francistown, 184
Frobenius, L., 152

Gaborone, 184
Game Pass, **81**, 186
Garlake, P., 187
gemsbok, 18, 34, 69
genitals, 106
geometric depictions, *see* entoptic phenomena
Giant's Castle, 186
giraffe, 34, 54
girls' puberty rituals, 119
Gold River Ranch, 187
graves, 21
grids, *see* entoptic phenomena
Guenther, M., 9, 28
gypsum, 18

haematite, 18
hair, 51, 55, 70, 72, 78, 90
    depictions of, **1, 20, 22, 28, 30a, 32a, 33c, 63, 73**

193

hallucinations
    after-images, 35, 68
    aural, 63, 68
    somatic, 68, 75, 76, 77, 78
    visual, 35, 60-67, 68, 91, 94, 133, 150, 155, **84a, 86c**
hallucinogens, 32, 60, 135
handprints, 8, 108-109, **50**
Harare, 187
hare, 13
hartebeest, 126, 132, **60a,79**
healing, see shamans, curing
heart, 54
Heinz, H-J., 132
hippopotamus, 138, **66c, 85e**
honeycombs, 63, 108, **27a, 28**
hoofprints, 102, 119, 154, **47b, 75**
Hopefield skull, 9
horns, 82, 120, 128
horse, 82, 147, **70**
Hottentots, see Khoikhoi
How, M., 19, 20
Howell, N., 28
human beings
    depictions of, 104-111
hunting, 48, 52, 104, 117, 119, 125, 138
    in trance, 101
huts, 38, 46, 134

idiosyncrasy
    in art, 73, 140
    in religion, 35, 73
infibulation, 52
    depictions of, **14, 19a, 21c, 35c, 38b, 48a, 51, 67b, 80, 86b**
Iron Age farmers, 8, 112, 142-145
    depictions of, **69**

jackal, 134, **64a**
Johannesburg, 188
juxtapositioning, 150

Kabwe skull, 9
/Kaggen, see Mantis
Kalahari Bushmen, 28, 35, 112, 134, 144, **3, 7, 12, 13**
Kalahari Desert, 11, 46, 144
Kalkoenkranz, 186
Kamberg, 81
Karoo, 16, **81**
kaross, 45, 51, 100
    depictions of, **14, 16a, 17, 20, 24, 30c, 31a, 39a, 41a, 46, 49a, 54, 67b, 72, 74, 75, 76a, 76b, 81**
Katz, R., 28, 34, 48, 70, 87, 132
Kenhardt, 27

Khoekhoe, see Khoikhoi
Khoikhoi, 9, 108, 142, 145
Khoisan, 8
Kimberley, 16, 22, 186
Klasies River Mouth cave, 21
knee, raised see postures
knobkierie, 145, **69, 86a**
!Kõ, 11, 132
Kromrivier, 186
Kruger National Park, 14, 187
kudu, 34, 126
    depictions of, 17, **60b, 87b**
!Kung, 9, 11, 13, 32, 44, 52, 59, 70, 72, 77, 87, 118, 119, 126, 127, 132, 136, 138

Landseer, E., 25
Langalibalele, 28
Lapalala Wilderness, 187
Lascaux, 21
Later Stone Age, 9
Lee, R., 28
legs, 102, 103
leopard, see felines
Lesotho, 19, 126, 185
lines, 55, 90, 154, **18, 22, 23, 28, 41a, 41b, 71, 80, 85a, 87a**
    from head, 72, 74, 82, 85, 136, **33, 65b**
    on faces, 80, 85, **15, 17, 19b, 20, 22, 24, 28, 29, 32d, 34a, 36a, 36b, 36c, 38a, 38b, 39a, 40, 45, 48a, 54, 72, 73, 76a, 80**
lions, see felines
Lloyd, L.C., 27, 28, 46
locusts, 34
louse, 13

Maack, R., 6, 7
Magaliesberg, 16
Maggs, T.M.O'C., 138
magic, see sympathetic magic
Malmesbury, 4
Malutis, 14, 17, 19, 21
manganese, 18
Mannsfeld, E., 152
Mantis, 13, 54, 116, 120, 125, 126, 129, 130, 135
Manyana, 184
Mapote, 19, 20
marriage rituals, 119
Marshall, L., 28, 32, 43, 48, 136
Martinshoek, 186
Maseru, 185
Matopo Hills, 187
Matsieng, 184
Maun, 184

194

McGregor Museum, 186, 188
meat, colours of, 126, 138
medicine man, see shaman
meerkats, 59, 120, 135
metaphors, 29, 31, 48, 118, 122, 154
    death, 30, 50-53, 59, 68, 153-154
    fight, 48, 58-59
    flight, 56-57, 116, 137
    rain, 92-99
    spoil, 29, 30, 32, 51, 68, 94, 128
    underwater, 30, 54-57, 68, 86, 88, 94, 116, 131, 140
    winking, 116
migraine, 60
milk, 94
Mlambonja Rock, 3, 13, 14, 18, 23, 25, 30, 36, 72, 182
mobile art, 21-23
Modderpoort, 187

Nama, 9
Namibia, 6, 8, 17, 21, 136, 185
Naron, 134
Natal, 145, 186-187
Natal Museum, 188
National Cultural History Museum, 188
National Monuments Act, 183
n//au, 32
Ndedema Gorge, 104
nose, 46, 80
    blood from, see blood, nasal
n/um, see potency

ochre, 18
Orange Free State, 134, 136, 138, 145, 187, 188
Orpen, J.M., 28-29, 51, 68, 69, 92, 128, 130, 152
ostrich, 135, 136, 147, **65a**
    eggshell beads, 114, 136
Oudtshoorn, 21
ox, 19, 94, 133
out-of-body travel, 32, 75, 88, 90, 118, 131, 132, 133, 136

Pager, H., 7, 104
paints, 18-19
Perlea capreolus, see rhebuck
perspective, 38, 150, 154
photography, 182
Pietermaritzburg, 188
poison, 52, 112
polymelia, see hallucinations, somatic
Pondomise, 19, 36
postures
    arms-back, 44, 67, 72, 77, 90, 116, 152, 153, **29,
31c, 32a, 32c, 33a, 34b, 41b, 45, 49b, 54, 67b, 74, 75**
    bending forward, 40, 44, 51, 152, **15, 16c, 17, 20, 21b, 24, 28, 29, 32a, 34a, 36b, 41a, 47a, 49b, 67**
    hand-to-nose, 48, 116, **19a, 28, 29, 45, 54, 69**
    kneeling, 72, 90, **14, 32, 45, 76b**
    pointing finger, 48, **19b, 19c**
    raised knee, 49, 80, 153, **19c**
    upheld hands, 42, **14, 16b, 16c, 43**
potency, supernatural, 32, 34, 42, 43, 44, 45, 46, 48, 59, 69, 70, 77, 90, 94, 106, 108, 117, 118, 119, 122, 126, 132, 147, 154
Potgieter, E.F., 131
pottery, 143
power, supernatural, see potency
preservation of rock art, 15, 17
Pretoria, 188

Qachasnek, 19
Qing, 28-30, 32, 51, 68, 92, 94, 125, 128, 129
quagga, 127
quills, 19
quiver, 100, 104, 114, **46, 48a, 53a, 81, 86b**
Qwanciqutshaa, 128, 130, 131

radiocarbon dating, see age of art
rain-animal, see shamans, rain-making
rain-making, see shamans
Redunca fulvorufula, see rhebuck
rhebuck, 128-129
    depictions of, **22, 28, 36c, 61, 74, 85d**
Reichel-Dolmatoff, R., 60
rhinoceros, 138, **66a**
rifles, 144, 146, **70**
rivers, 29, 54
rock shelters, 14, 15, 36
Rodin, A., 24

San, see Bushmen
sap, 19
Schaapplaats, 187
schizophrenia, 75
Sealy, J., 138
serpents, 13, 34, 63, 67, 88, 130-131, 134, 152
    depictions of, **27b, 29, 47b, 62**
shamans, 12, 30, **12, 13**
    Bushmen words for, 32
    control of animals, 32, 36, 48, 100-103, 118, 128
    curing, 32, 36, 108, 118
    rain-making, 32, 36, 54, 56-57, 92-99, 128, 138,
sheep, 8, 9, 142, 145, 147, **68a**
shields, 145, **69**
Shostak, M., 28

195

sickness, 32
Siegel, R., 60
Silberbauer, G., 28
silica, 18
Singer, R., 21
Smuts, J.C., 6, 7
snakes, *see* serpents
snoring power, *see* trance dance
songs, 32
South African Museum, 188
spears, 133, 145, **69**
specularite, 18
spine, 32, 70, 77, 87, 95
spirit animals, 34, 85
spirits of the dead, 13, 30, 32, 34
spirit world, 34, 35, 36, 49, 50, 53, 75, 86, 91, 94, 100, 105, 119, 141, 150, 155
Spitzkoppe, 185
spoil, *see* metaphors
spoor, *see* hoofprints
springbok, 18, 48, 100, 129, 134
sternum, 77
stomach, 48, 77
    see also postures, bending forward
Stow, G.W., 8, 12, 152
superimposition, 90, 148-150
Swaziland, 187
sympathetic magic, 23-24
synaesthesia, 70, 78, 87

technique
    engravings, 19-20
    learning, 20
    paintings, 18-19
teeth, 85, **38b, 76b**
Thackeray, A. and F., 22
Theal, G.M., 4
therianthropes, 7, 22, 29, 51, 54, 59, 68, 72, 77, 78, 82, 88, 95, 128, 136, 138
    depictions of, **8b, 20, 21b, 22, 24, 30-32, 35a, 37b, 38b, 39a, 40, 43, 47a, 72, 73, 74, 76, 80, 81, 82a, 82b, 84a, b, c, 87e**
Tindall, H., 4
Tobias, P.V., 28
Trafalgar Square, 25
trance, 32, 34
    experience, 68-91
    stages of, 60-67
    inducing of, 32, 60
trance-buck, 72-73, 85, 90, 149
    depictions of, **1, 31c, 32, 45, 73**
Transvaal, 17, 131, 136, 187
trembling, 32, 100

Tsodilo Hills, 11, 184
tufted sticks, 114, **53c, 76a**
Tukano, 60, 62
Tungus, 30
turtles, 88, 140, **40**
tusks, 66, 67, 85, 130
    depictions of, **29, 62, 63, 73, 76a, 76b**
Twyfelfontein, 185

underwater, *see* metaphors
Upper Palaeolithic art, 21, 23
urine, 19

vandalism, 184
Van der Merwe, N., 21
Van Riebeeck, J., 4
Van Riet Lowe, C., 14
Vinnicombe, P., 128
visions, *see* hallucinations, visual
Von Daniken, E., 6
vortex, *see* entopic phenomena
vulture, 13

waist, 106
Waterberg, 14, 108
waterhole, 54, 57, 88, 116
Wendt, E., 21
White Lady of the Brandberg, 6-7, 25, 185, **2**
Whitley, D., 22
Wiessner, P., 28
wildebeest, 126-127, **60b**
Wilmsen, E., 132
Windhoek, 185
winking, *see* metaphors, winking
Wintervogel, J., 4
witches, mediaeval, 56
women, 31, 42, 46, 105, 136
    depictions of, **14, 16a, 18, 28, 48b, 53e, 67b, 71, 76a**
Wonderwerk cave, 22
    art from, **9**
Wymer, J., 21

/Xam, 11, 18, 27, 28, 32, 40, 44, 46, 51, 54, 59, 69, 70, 92, 94, 106, 108, 112, 117, 118, 129, 132, 135, 136
//Xegwi, 130
Xhosa, 36

zebra, 34
    depictions of, 20, 22, **9a**
zigzags, *see* entopic phenomena
Zimbabwe, 17, 187
Zu/'hoasi, *see* !Kung

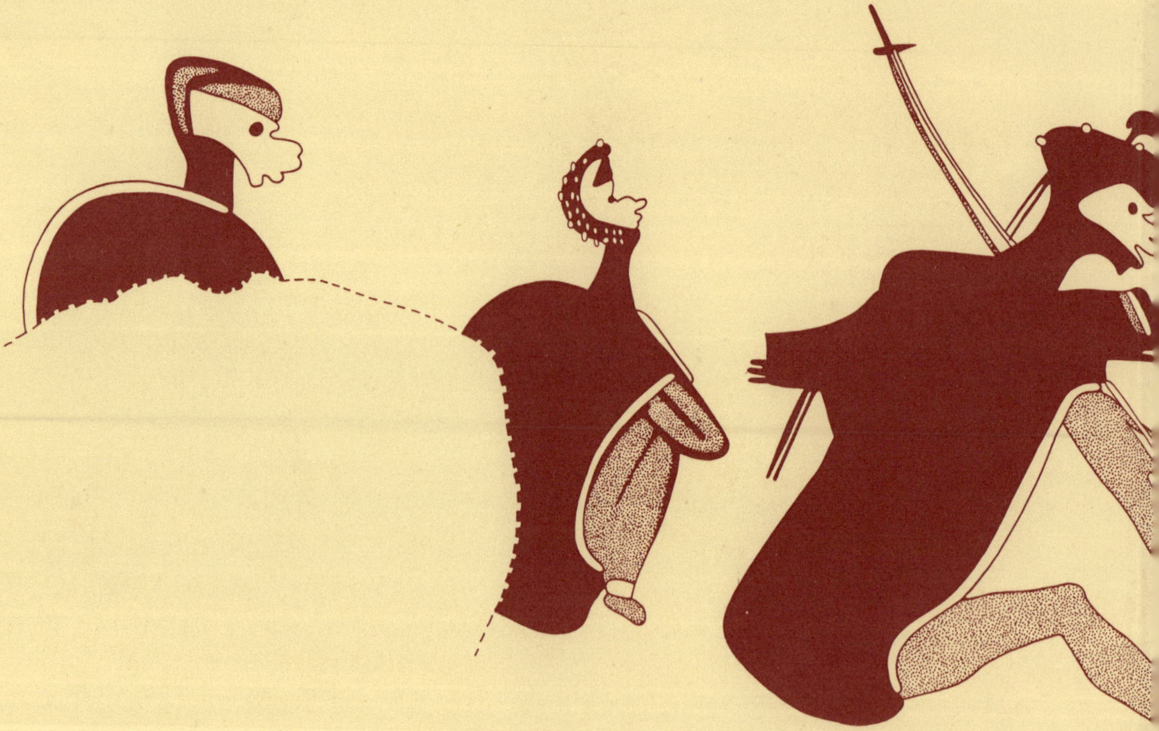